THE POWER OF ACTION

DO IT NOW

DANIEL WALTER

THE POWER OF ACTION: Do It Now
by Daniel Walter

© **Copyright 2023 by Daniel Walter**

All Rights Reserved.

No part of this publication may be reproduced, distributed, or transmitted in any form or by any means, including photocopying, recording, or other electronic or mechanical methods, without the prior written permission of the publisher, except in the case of brief quotations embodied in reviews and certain other noncommercial uses permitted by copyright law.

Disclaimer: This book is designed to provide accurate and authoritative information in regard to the subject matter covered. By its sale, neither the publisher nor the author is engaged in rendering psychological or other professional services. If expert assistance or counseling is needed, the services of a competent professional should be sought

ISBN: 979-8877923744

ALSO BY DANIEL WALTER

*The Power of Discipline: How to Use Self-Control
and Mental Toughness to Achieve Your Goals*

*How to Stop Procrastinating: Powerful Strategies
to Overcome Laziness and Multiply Your Time*

Habits for Success: How to Change Your Life One Step at a Time

CONTENTS

Introduction 7
Your Free Gift – Master Your Morning 15
Chapter 1: The Awakening: Self-Awareness and Acknowledging Your Weakness 21
Chapter 2: Ditch the Victim Mentality: Success Is for Everyone 41
Chapter 3: It Starts in the Mind: Think and Grow Rich ... 63
Chapter 4: The Power of Order: Get Your House Organized 103
Chapter 5: Write the Vision and Make It Plain: Goal-Setting with a Purpose 122
Chapter 6: Ditch the Distractions: How to Maintain Your Focus 131
Chapter 7: Go All Out: Forget About Work-Life Balance for Now 146
Chapter 8: Motivation Is Not Enough: How to Keep Going When You Don't Feel It 153
Chapter 9: Developing Discipline: Nothing Happens Without Self-Discipline 174
Chapter 10: Creating Momentum: Tap Into the Snowball Effect 199
Chapter 11: Friends No More: You Can't Take Everyone to the Top 209

Chapter 12: Success Is Not Temporary: How to Make
 Success a Lifestyle 242
Chapter 13: Embracing Discomfort: Get Comfortable
 with Being Uncomfortable 262
Chapter 14: Dealing with Disappointment:
 The Power of Patience 272
Chapter 15: One Step at a Time: Celebrate Your
 Small Wins 293
Conclusion 300

INTRODUCTION

*"In order to carry a positive action,
we must develop here a positive vision."*
—Dali Lama

According to research, 92% of people who set goals fail to achieve them. A Gallup poll discovered that 85% of people hate their jobs, and the World Happiness Report finds that negative emotions are on the rise worldwide. I believe these statistics are all connected. People hate their jobs because there is something deep within them that knows there is more to life than working in a job they can't stand and struggling to pay bills. We set goals because we want to create the life we know we deserve. But we fail to achieve those goals because we don't know how to, and then negative emotions such as sadness, depression, and frustration overtake us because we just can't seem to get it right. It's like one big vicious circle that people can't get out of and it's becoming unbearable.

But there is light at the end of the tunnel if you will allow me to lead you there. Why do I believe there is hope? Because five years ago, I was a part of the three statistics I just mentioned. I worked as an accounts manager for a telecommunications company and I hated my job with a passion. I was one of those people who lived for the weekends and dreaded Mondays. I had to psych myself up every morning before I went into the office, and I walked around with a fake smile on my face all day because there really wasn't anything to smile about. I wasn't happy to be there.

I always knew I wanted to be an author, and every year for seven years I made a New Year's resolution to write a book, but it never happened. Every year, I became more and more disgusted with myself for failing to achieve my goals. My confidence was at an all-time low, and I buried my sadness by filling my time with mindless activities and associating with people who were just as miserable as me.

My life changed one warm summer's day after speaking to an old man called Mr. Hamilton who lived down the street from me. He always sat on his porch in a rocking chair reading the book *Think and Grow Rich* by Napoleon Hill. He said he had been reading the same book for 45 years. He had more or less memorized it word for word and could quote entire pages. He said that was the only book anyone ever needed to read in order to succeed in life. If he was outside when I passed by, I would join him on his porch and have a chat. His favorite topic of conversation was the importance of creating the life you desire. He had wanted to get into real estate, but once he'd started a family, his main concern had become keeping a roof over their heads and food on the table. He didn't want to risk investing his life savings into something that might not work, so he abandoned his dreams and chose the safe road.

Mr. Hamilton believed that since he had not managed to achieve his dreams, his mission in life was to teach young people not to allow fear to hold them back from becoming successful. During our last conversation, he said, "On your gravestone there will be two dates: the day you were born, and the day you died. There will be a dash in the middle of those dates. What you do during that time is up to you. Please do something with your life." Mr. Hamilton died that evening and I never saw him again. His words stuck with me, though, so I went and bought the book *Think and Grow Rich*. I had attempted to read several self-help books over the years and failed, but I read that book in one evening and something clicked. I became more determined than ever to turn my dreams into a reality.

Today, I am a successful best-selling author, public speaker, and philanthropist. I travel the world teaching people how to apply the principles of success, and I've never been so fulfilled and satisfied with life. I wrote this book because I understand exactly how you feel. Five years ago, I was you. I've walked in your shoes, and I can tell you with confidence that there is a way out. When I started this journey, one of the things I struggled with the most was taking action—which is the most important component of the journey, because without action, nothing gets done. But the more I learned and applied the success principles I read about, the easier it became for me to take action. And that's what I want to share with you. Here's a sneak peek into what you can expect to learn in this book:

- A deep dive into the importance of self-awareness
- How to acknowledge and overcome your weaknesses
- Strategies to motivate yourself and build momentum
- Why fear is holding you back from success
- The benefits of setting specific goals
- How to enjoy the process and celebrate your wins

If you diligently apply the strategies found in this book, and refuse to give up on your dreams, I can guarantee you will be successful. It takes courage to decide that it's time to change your life, and I applaud you for that. With that being said, it's time to take the first action step on your journey, and read the first chapter of this book.

JOIN OUR PRODUCTIVITY GROUP

In order to maximize the value you receive from this book, I highly encourage you to join our tight-knit community on Facebook. Here you will be able to connect and share productivity strategies in order to continue your growth.

It would be great to connect with you there,

Daniel Walter

To Join, Visit:
www.pristinepublish.com/focusgroup

DOWNLOAD THE AUDIO VERSION OF THIS BOOK FREE

If you love listening to audiobooks on the go or would enjoy a narration as you read along, I have great news for you. You can download the audiobook version of *The Power of Action* for FREE (regular price $14.95) just by signing up for a FREE 30-day Audible trial!

Visit: www.pristinepublish.com/audiobooks

YOUR FREE GIFT – MASTER YOUR MORNING

Just thinking about the word "morning" can put a bad taste in people's mouths. A recent study found that one in four Americans hit the snooze button twice before getting out of bed. Forty-nine percent of the same sample stated that waking up late is the main reason they are always late.

In other words, too many of us struggle with productivity, and there are very few people who jump out of bed as soon as their alarm goes off, excited about starting the day.

I want you to take a couple of minutes and think about what your morning usually looks like…

So you don't feel alone in this, I'll start with what mine looked like a little less than three years ago.

- Set my alarm for 6:00 a.m. Hit the snooze button until 7:00 a.m.
- Jump out of bed, shower, get dressed and run out the door
- Get a McDonald's breakfast and eat it on my way to work
- Shout at the drivers on the road because it's their fault I woke up an hour late
- Get to work with two minutes to spare
- Sit at my desk stuffing my face with coffee and snacks all morning to keep my energy levels up

But then I learned about the power of a consistent morning routine—and my life changed. I went from thinking I'd never achieve my dreams, to seeing them slowly manifest while I was becoming confident that I could have anything I set my mind to. Let me start by explaining how healthy morning routines are created and why they make us more productive.

If I had to use an alternative word for "routine," I'd use the word "freedom" because that's what it gives us. Think about it like this: what's the first thing you do when you wake up in the morning? Most of you are going to say, "Brush my teeth." That's because it's a habit. Since childhood, we've been trained to brush our teeth as soon as we get out of bed in the morning, so we don't even think about it; we just do it. When you get in your car every morning to go to work, do you sit there thinking about how you're going to drive your vehicle? No, you just put your foot on the accelerator and go because it's a habit. But when you were first learning to drive, your driving instructor had to tell you what to do, and you had to think carefully about it when you were on the road. It may have taken a while, but you got there in the end, didn't you?

Establishing a morning routine works in the same way. Once it becomes a habit, and you're powering through your routine on autopilot, it will give you freedom because you will no longer struggle to succeed.

When we get down to basics, routines are the foundation of life; everything you do is routine, even if you don't think it is. Your bad morning habits of getting up late and having breakfast on the go have become a routine. The way you style your hair is a routine; the location you leave your shoes when you return home is a routine. Can you see my point? Everything is about routine.

The problem is that your current routines aren't doing you any favors. In fact, they're hindering you. Everything you do in the morning has become an enemy of progress, and the longer you continue living this way, the longer your success will be delayed. If you're anything like me, you probably don't know where to start when it comes to establishing a morning routine. I had no idea what I was doing when I started on this journey, but I had some good people in my life who gave me step-by-step instructions. And now I want to give them to you.

In my bonus e-book, *Master Your Morning,* you will learn about the seven habits you need to apply to become that person who jumps out of bed every morning raring to go. Here are three of them:

1. **A Bedtime Routine:** Sleep is one of the most important things you'll do every evening. Sleep is wonderful, and we all love sleeping—which is the main reason so many of you hit the snooze button every morning! You've probably heard that healthy adults need eight hours of sleep a night, right? Arguably, this is true, but what you may not know is that the *quality* of your sleep is more important than the *quantity*. Do you wake up feeling drained and tired no matter how many hours of sleep you get? That's because you're not getting good-quality sleep. And the reason for this is that you've got a terrible nighttime routine.

1. **Wake Up Early:** As you've just read, it's the quality of your sleep that will determine whether you wake up refreshed or not. The first step to dropping the terrible habit of smashing the snooze button every morning is establishing a good bedtime routine so you wake up

feeling refreshed and energized. Waking up early is an essential habit to cultivate if you want to succeed because it gives you a head start on the day.

1. **No Electronics:** Did you know that smartphone addiction is a real thing? I was addicted to my phone, and I had zero awareness of it. Every time it pinged, I would check to see who was messaging me, and I was always on social media. If you're going to get anywhere in life, kicking this habit is essential—and I'll show you how to do it.

Just by pondering these three habits, can you see where you're going wrong? That's just a snippet of what's in store for you in *Master Your Morning*. You will have access to an abundance of helpful information that will kickstart your journey toward success and get you one step closer to living your dream life.

If you've got to that point where you're sick and tired of being sick and tired, this book is for you. It will equip you with everything you need to become more productive and start taking control of your life instead of letting life control *you*!

Get *Master Your Morning* for Free by Visiting

www.pristinepublish.com/morningbonus

CHAPTER 1:

THE AWAKENING: SELF-AWARENESS AND ACKNOWLEDGING YOUR WEAKNESS

"To know yourself, you must sacrifice the illusion that you already do."
—Vironika Tugaleva

Everyone loves sleeping. There's nothing like that awesome warm feeling when you're tucked under a duvet getting the rest your body craves so much. But when that alarm goes off, the first thing most people do is reach up and shut it off. Why? Because you've been jolted out of your slumber and you have absolutely no desire to get out of bed. You are engulfed in that comfortable feeling, and if you could stay there forever you would. However, whether it's work, the kids, or life, you have no choice but to get up.

The same is true when one has a spiritual awakening. Most people are sleepwalking; they live on autopilot, doing everything society has programmed them to do. You go to school, get an education, get a job, and work until retirement—during which time you might have snippets of fulfilment, but deep down, there is a massive void you don't know how to fill. You see, humans are made up of body, mind, and spirit. We are aware of our bodies, and our minds, but the spirit, the inner part of you that knows all things, most people are unaware of. As far as I'm concerned, the spirit is the most important part of us, but it is never fully activated because we live in such a superficial world. We've been taught to be so focused on our outer appearance that our inner being is totally neglected. But every so often, an alarm bell rings, whether it's through a book we read, a podcast we listened to, or a film we watched, and we get the feeling that there is more to life than we are currently living. However, because we are so comfortable in our slumber, we hit the snooze button and go back to sleep. There are very few people who hear the alarm bell and get up, which is why only 1% of the population owns half of the world's wealth. The question is, what does it take to enable you to arise from your slumber? There are several answers to this question, and one of them is self-awareness.

What Is Self-Awareness?

Self-awareness is a deep concept that involves having the ability to understand yourself. It involves more than self-recognition; introspection is the foundation of self-awareness. Self-awareness means being able to critically evaluate your thoughts, actions, and emotions. It requires a person to have a deep understanding of their personal values, strengths, weaknesses, and motivations.

This skill is required for personal development, but it also plays an important role in how people interact with each other.

At the center of self-awareness is the ability to navigate one's internal state. A person who engages in the practice of self-reflection is capable of identifying thought patterns and the behaviors that manifest from them, which assists in developing a clearer picture of their identity and personality. It's important to mention that once a person becomes self-aware, it does not necessarily mean that the negative things they've learned about themselves are fixed. Through life experiences, reflection, and learning, people grow, change, and evolve.

Self-awareness also involves being able to identify and manage emotions. Having the ability to manage one's emotions is referred to as "emotional intelligence." This skill gives people an advantage in social situations because they are capable of accurately reading rooms and people. Emotionally intelligent people are more empathetic, which gives them the ability to communicate on a deeper level and build stronger relationships.

Understanding your strengths and weaknesses is another important component of self-awareness. A person who knows their strengths is confident in their abilities and works to keep improving them. The individual who understands their weaknesses (more on that shortly) does not allow those weaknesses to dominate their lives. Instead, they either work on improving them, or they simply accept that there are certain things they are just not good at. Either way, it's a win-win situation when you understand your weaknesses because you are clear on what to do, and what not to do.

Finally, self-awareness is also about understanding how your behavior impacts others. It ensures that you think before you speak so your words do not cause offense. Before making decisions, you think about how your actions will affect those involved in the situation. Self-aware people are also extremely humble and have no problem admitting when they are wrong.

How to Develop Self-Awareness

If you feel that you lack self-awareness, not to worry—you can develop it. Here are some tips to help you develop self-awareness:

Identify Your Personal Values: Everyone has personal values. You may never have articulated them, but they are basically how you live your life. They are the principles and beliefs that shape your decisions and actions. Your personal values are typically developed during childhood, as you grow into adulthood, and through your experiences. Your personal values will influence things such as the relationships you choose, the career you opt for, and the overall direction your life will take. Therefore, having a clear understanding of your personal values is essential. By defining your personal values, you connect with the things that are most important to you. Here are some tips on how to identify your personal values. You will need a pen and a notebook for this.

- **Happy Moments:** Think about the times in your life when you were the happiest. Come up with examples from your childhood, different relationships you've had, and your career.

- **Proud Moments:** Think about the times in your life when you were most proud. Again, use examples from your childhood, different relationships you've had, and your career. What was it that made you proud? Were there other people involved, and if so, did they share the moment with you? What were the main factors that contributed to these proud moments?

- **Satisfied and Fulfilled:** Think about times when you were the most satisfied and fulfilled. Come up with more recent examples in your career and personal life. What desire or need was fulfilled? Why did these experiences add meaning to your life? Were there any other factors that added to these feelings of fulfilment?

- **Your Main Values:** Based on the experiences you have come up with—happy, proud, satisfied and fulfilled moments—why did you remember each experience? Why were they important to you? Try and come up with at least 10 main values.

- **Prioritize Your Values:** As mentioned, your values have an effect on the decisions you make. Therefore, it is essential that you are aware of the values that are most important to you. Look at the first two values on the list you made above, and ask yourself, "If I had to make a choice, which one of these values would I choose?" Context is always going to have an effect on your decisions; therefore, imagine a scenario where you would need to make such a choice. For example, say the first two values on your list are "generosity" and "financial stability." Imagine one of your friends is going through a rough patch and they ask to borrow some money. Although you value generosity, you are not financially stable, and lending your friend money would set you back. In this instance, financial stability would be more important than generosity. Go through your list making up scenarios until you've numbered the list from 1-10.

- **Personal Alignment:** Go through your list and determine whether these values are in alignment with your life. Ask yourself whether these values give you a sense of pride. How would you feel about telling the people closest to you, and those you admire and respect, about your personal values? Would you stand by these values even if they were not popular?

When you take your personal values into consideration when making a decision, you will maintain your integrity because you are doing what you know is right, and what is true to your heart. In this way, you can approach decisions with clarity and confidence. You can also be confident that the decisions you make are the best for your present and future satisfaction and happiness. It won't always be easy when prioritizing your personal values during the decision-making process; however, it will serve you well in the long run.

Additional Tips for Defining Your Personal Values

- Next to each value, write down what it means to you—why it matters and what it stands for.
- Be short and concise with your definitions.
- Use your own words so you can truly connect with them.
- Embrace your authenticity and don't write down values because of external influences.
- Take your core beliefs into consideration and don't compromise on them.

Practice Journaling: Journaling involves setting time aside on a regular basis to write about your emotions, feelings, and thoughts. It helps you self-reflect and problem-solve. Journaling is very therapeutic, and research suggests there are several benefits to it such as improving your mental health, strengthening the immune system, and helping to relieve stress and anxiety. Here are some tips on how to get started with journaling:

- **Get a Notepad:** Don't journal on random sheets of paper; instead, buy a notepad specifically for journaling.

- **Choose a Time:** You don't need to journal every day unless you want to. But the key is to be consistent. Whether you are going to journal every day, twice a week, or once a week, choose the best time of day and stick to it.

- **No Distractions:** Turn off your phone, the TV, the radio, and any other form of digital distractions before you start journaling. Your environment should be as peaceful as possible so you can focus on what you are writing.

- **Write Freely:** Spelling and grammar are irrelevant when it comes to journaling, so just write. As long as you can read what you write, that's all that matters.

I'm a writer, so I found journaling very easy, but for those of you who have no idea where to start, here are some journal prompts to help you out:

- Describe an incident that occurred during your day that made you feel joyful.

- Is there anything you are grateful for in this present moment?

- Think about a challenge you've had recently. What did you learn from it?
- What goals do you want to accomplish in the next 30 days?
- Are there any hobbies and skills you would like to develop and why?
- Have you had any emotional challenges recently? How did you navigate them and what did they teach you about yourself?
- What practices or activities give you peace and improve your mood?
- What have you accomplished recently? What emotions did you experience?
- What situations trigger anxiety and stress in you and why?
- Who are the people in your life that you trust the most and why? How can you strengthen the emotional connections you have with these people?
- What self-care practices do you enjoy the most and why? How can you incorporate more of them into your life?
- Who is your role model? What qualities do you admire about this person?
- What are the things that make you angry and why?
- What can you do to make the world a better place?
- Think about the three biggest mistakes you have made in life. How did they affect you?

Develop a Growth Mindset: Psychologist Carol Dweck coined the term "growth mindset." A person with a growth mindset believes that their intelligence and abilities can be improved through learning, hard work, and dedication. They push through adversities and see the difficulties of life as opportunities to learn something new and grow. On the other hand, a person with a fixed mindset believes that people are born with a certain level of skill and intelligence and there is nothing that can be done to change it. You can develop a growth mindset by doing the following:

- **Recognize a Fixed Mindset:** Before you can develop a growth mindset, you must be aware that you have a fixed mindset. When you find something difficult, do you keep trying, or do you give up because you don't believe you will get any better at it? When you run into an obstacle, do you see it as an opportunity for growth, or do you complain and moan that it's hindering your progress? These are all ways that a person with a fixed mindset thinks. Pay attention to your thought process the next time you run into a challenge.

- **Embrace Failure:** Failure is not a dead end; it is a part of the process. All successful people fail before they succeed. Thomas Edison attempted to make the bamboo filament to improve the lightbulb 2,774 times before he succeeded. During an interview, he let the interviewer know that he was willing to keep trying until he got it right by saying, "I have not failed. I've just found 10,000 ways that won't work." When things are not going your way, do what Thomas Edison did and find another way of achieving your goal, no matter how long it takes.

- **Embrace Challenges:** Like failure, view the challenges that life throws at you as an opportunity for growth. Growth comes by venturing out of your comfort zone; while it doesn't feel good to be stretched and challenged, by embracing it, you will come out on the other side better and stronger.

- **Value Hard Work:** Hard work is the engine that propels growth. You can be the most talented person in the world, but if you are not prepared to put the work in, you won't get very far. When you are working on your goals, your progress might seem slow, but eventually, you will reap the rewards for your efforts.

- **Keep Learning:** The desire to learn is essential for a growth mindset because that's how you get better at something. Learning can take place in many forms including reading, taking courses, and watching instructional videos.

- **Be Persistent:** Persistence is key when it comes to developing a growth mindset because whatever you are trying to achieve is not going to happen overnight. There are going to be setbacks, difficulties, and things that will make you feel very uncomfortable. Most people give up when the going gets tough because it's easier to go back to what they know. But a person with a growth mindset will embrace the discomfort and keep going until they have reached their goal.

- **Choose Your Friends Wisely:** If you are surrounded by people with a fixed mindset, they will make it very difficult for you to make the changes you need to make to adopt a growth mindset. While it's easier said than done to ditch the people you've probably known for years, you will need to distance yourself from them. While you're all excited about your personal development journey and will want them to accompany you, they will tell you it's a waste of time. The more they keep reminding you that you are not going to succeed at what you're doing, the easier it will be for you to give up when things get hard. Think about it like this: Imagine you are standing on top of a table, your friends are on the ground, and you stretch out your hand to help pull them up. Guess what's going to happen? Gravity will ensure that they pull you down before you can pull them up. If they want to get on your level, they will find their own way there—you won't need to convince them. However, if they are not ready to embrace this new mindset, they will pull you right back down to the bottom of the mountain.

- **Seek Feedback:** Individuals with a growth mindset love constructive criticism. They don't get offended because it gives them the opportunity to improve. Constructive criticism can come from your superiors at work, your partner, friends, or family members. Regardless of where it comes from, embrace it and make the necessary changes to improve.

Embrace Vulnerability: It is not uncommon for people to find it difficult to embrace vulnerability. Being vulnerable is about being transparent with your thoughts, emotions, and actions. It's about being your authentic self even though you know you could get hurt. Being vulnerable with your loved ones allows you to connect with them on a deeper level. To start embracing your vulnerability, do this:

- **Be Yourself:** Society has tricked us into believing we can't be ourselves, that we have to look and act a certain way to be accepted and liked. The media does a wonderful job of highlighting the differences between those who are admired and those who are not. We are constantly bombarded with indirect messages about what is considered socially acceptable. As a result, people feel that they need to change themselves in order to be accepted. Embracing vulnerability requires you to be yourself because in doing so, you are okay with knowing that not everyone is going to like you. You can make this process a lot easier by reminding yourself that no matter how nice and polished you are, no matter how much you conform to society's standards, you can't please everyone, and there are always going to be people who are not going to like you. Once you accept this fact, you will free yourself from the shackles of conformity.

- **Learn and Grow:** Learn about yourself and do the work required to grow. By gaining a better understanding of who you are and acknowledging the parts of you that you don't like, you can do what is necessary to make changes. Most people keep these parts about themselves buried because they are too painful to confront. However, the first step in the direction of transformation is admitting you have a problem. Once the problem has been diagnosed, you can start working on the solution.

- **Embrace Your Feelings:** For some people, it is easier to hide their feelings instead of being honest about them. However, burying your feelings is not good for your health. Emotions are designed to be released from the body, and if they are not, they will make you both mentally and physically ill. By embracing your feelings, you accept them for what they are, no matter how uncomfortable they make you feel. When you accept your emotions and work through them, they will no longer have any power over you.

- **Be Adventurous:** People who embrace their vulnerability are free-spirited; they enjoy getting out in the world and having new experiences because they don't mind taking risks. You might waste money, or you could have a terrible time, but to those who embrace their vulnerability, an experience is an experience whether it was good or bad. You can't go through life trying to avoid bad experiences; instead, get out there and live.

- **Become Indifferent:** Worrying about what other people think about you is a waste of time because the truth is, you will never really know. There are very few people who will tell you what they really think about you because that's not proper social etiquette. My friend once sent me a cute video of a little girl being recorded by her mom practicing how she was going to be nice to the other kids at the party she was about to attend. This child was known for telling people that she didn't like them, and in the video, the mom asks, "What are you going to say when you go to Auntie Jackie's party? The child replied very slowly, "I DON'T LIKE YOU." The mother asked her the question three times, and she eventually said, "I LIKE YOU" in the same robotic voice. She then said, "But the truth is, I don't like you!" Children have no filter, and it's up to their parents to train them how to navigate the world. The average adult has a filter, and in most cases, they are going to be polite and friendly even if they don't like you. Since you are not telepathic and can't read minds, there is no point worrying about another person's opinion of you.

- **Practice Self-Compassion:** Be kind to yourself on your journey to embracing vulnerability because it isn't easy. You will find that your insecurities will rise, and you won't always be in the best of moods, but that's okay. If you let these feelings overwhelm you, they can have a negative effect on your life. You will start doubting yourself, questioning whether you are doing the right thing, and becoming critical of your flaws. When you start going through this, remember that it's normal to feel this way.

Recently, self-compassion has become an important part of mental health discussions and emotional well-being because psychologists and counselors have realized that people are very hard on themselves when life throws them challenges. According to Dr Julia Breines, it is important that we are able to forgive ourselves for the mistakes we make because everyone makes mistakes, and there are no perfect people in the world. Her studies have found that the inability to forgive oneself is linked to alcohol abuse, eating disorders, and suicide attempts. However, those who have embraced self-compassion seem to be able to handle stress better. Instead of dwelling on their problems, they accept that adversity is a part of life and don't allow negative circumstances to overwhelm them.

Everyone has flaws and insecurities, and it's not something you should be ashamed of. By being open and honest about your struggles, you give people permission to be open and honest about theirs, which helps to build stronger connections with your friends and loved ones. Living your best life means being authentic and operating in your personal truth. By getting to know every part of yourself and putting that version of you on display, you will learn to have a true appreciation for who you really are, flaws and all.

How to Recognize Your Weaknesses

When I started on my personal development journey, I had to accept that I was in the position I was in (more on that later) because of the decisions I had made. I had no one to blame for how my life had turned out but myself. My biggest weakness was procrastination; I had so many goals I wanted to achieve, but year after year, nothing was getting done because I was twiddling my thumbs. It wasn't until I got real with myself that things started changing for me. A major part of the awakening is accepting that the things you are struggling with are holding you back. A lot of people don't like this stage because it's easier to blame everyone else for your problems. My biggest excuse was that I was depressed because of a failed relationship. My partner cheated on me, and it messed me up big time. But after a lot of therapy and inner work, I accepted that the trauma people inflict on us is not our fault; we didn't do anything to deserve such treatment. However, healing is our responsibility. Regardless of the negative circumstances life has thrown at you, no one can heal you but you. The perpetrators have long gone on with their lives; they are not thinking about you, and waiting for them to apologize or do what needs to be done to repay you is a waste of time. Once you accept that you are the only person holding yourself back, life will become a lot easier. In this section, you will learn how to recognize your weaknesses.

Self-Reflection: Self-reflection involves evaluating your thoughts, emotions, and behavior. Basically, it's about analyzing why you do the things you do, and why you feel the way you do. Examining your life in this way might seem overwhelming because things are not going the way you had hoped, or you may just be so busy that you simply don't have the time for it. But if you want to change your life, it's important that you hit the pause button because there is so much value in self-reflection. It will help you identify what is working for you and what isn't. A part of understanding your weaknesses is getting to know yourself better, and self-reflection will help you accomplish this. Here are some questions to consider:

- What worries or fears give me sleepless nights?
- Is there anything in my life that I'm taking for granted?
- What parts of my life am I fully satisfied with?
- What parts of my life am I unsatisfied with?
- Do I have a positive outlook on life? If not, what can I do to create one?
- How can I improve my mental health?
- What worries me about the future?
- If I was to die tomorrow, how would I want my loved ones to remember me?

- What is most important to me?
- When was the last time I stepped out of my comfort zone?
- Who has made the biggest impact on my life?
- When was the last time a person was kind to me and how did it make me feel?
- What would I prefer to live with—failing at my goals or never trying?
- If I could change any aspect of my personality, what would it be?
- Why do I care about what others think about me?
- Is there anyone I trust enough to put my life in their hands?

Monitor Your Thoughts: More about thoughts in Chapter 3; however, when it comes to identifying your weaknesses, your thoughts play a major role because they govern your actions. Whatever you think about will manifest in your behavior. Therefore, paying attention to your thoughts will give you insight into your weaknesses. However, it's important to mention that it's difficult to monitor your thoughts because most of our thinking takes place on autopilot. For the most part, you are not paying attention to what you are thinking about. But it *is* possible to monitor your thoughts. Here's how:

- Make a conscious decision to monitor your thoughts by scheduling a time during the day to do so; for example, it could be first thing in the morning, or just before you go to bed.

- Find a quiet place and set a timer for 15 minutes. Get a pen and notepad, bring awareness to your thoughts and write them down.

- When 15 minutes are up, read over your thoughts and reflect on what you have been thinking about. Consider whether there was a purpose behind your thoughts. How did they make you feel? Did you have any positive thoughts? Did you have any negative thoughts?

- At the end of the first week, read through your thoughts and identify any patterns.

QUESTIONS TO IDENTIFY YOUR WEAKNESSES

Get a notebook and pen, find a quiet location where you won't be disturbed, and ask yourself the following questions:

- What bad habits do you have that prevent you from achieving your goals?

- What personality traits do you have that are holding you back from achieving your goals?

- In what areas do you lack confidence?

- What things do you avoid because they make you feel uncomfortable?

- Are there any situations where you find it difficult to communicate assertively?

- Do you find it difficult to maintain balance in your life?

- Is there anyone you are holding a grudge against because of the things they have done to you in the past?

- Do you have any bad habits that are hindering your relationships?

- Do you have any bad habits that are hindering your personal growth?

- Have your friends or family pointed out character flaws in you?

- When do you lack discipline and feel unmotivated?

S.W.O.T Analysis: An effective way to identify your weaknesses is to use the S.W.O.T analysis method. The letters S.W.O.T stand for *Strengths, Weaknesses, Opportunities, Threats*. It is typically used by organizations, but individuals can also use it for personal development. Here's how to do so:

- **Identify Your Strengths:** What positive attributes do you have? They can be personal qualities, skills, and/or knowledge. What are your most important values? What accomplishments are you the most proud of? Consider the things that people compliment you on the most. List any qualities that help you or others become better people.

- **Identify Your Weaknesses:** What negative attributes do you have? What areas of your life need improvement? Do you have any bad habits that are preventing you from achieving your goals or that are creating barriers to your personal development? Are there tasks you avoid because you don't think you're very good at them? What do your friends, family members, and co-workers perceive as your weaknesses? What negative personality traits do you have?

- **Identify Opportunities:** Are there any industry trends you can take advantage of? Are there any free courses on offer? Are there any mentors offering their services? Are there any networking events taking place?

- **Identify Threats:** Are you facing any obstacles at the moment? Do you have any enemies at work or in your personal life? Is technology threatening your job?

Once you have created your S.W.O.T analysis, you can use it as a map to guide you as you do the work required to improve your weaknesses.

This chapter should have been an eye-opener for you, and it might take a while for everything to truly sink in. The awakening is difficult and it requires doing some serious soul-searching. There are a lot of things you are not going to like, and that's okay. As long as you are serious about changing your life, and you're willing to do the work required to create the life you desire, you will achieve everything you set out to. You've got over the hardest part of this journey. In Chapter 2, you will learn all about how to ditch the victim mentality.

CHAPTER 2:

DITCH THE VICTIM MENTALITY: SUCCESS IS FOR EVERYONE

"Those with a perpetual victim mindset tend to create the situations from which they suffer."
—Steve Maraboli

Do you always feel as if the world is out to get you? Or that you don't have control over the things that happen to you? Or do you feel that no matter how hard you try, you seem to attract negative situations? If you're constantly blaming other people for the bad things that happen to you, you may suffer from a victim mentality. It's a mindset that makes you feel completely powerless over your life and keeps you stuck in a cycle of defeat. I used to have a victim mentality, and it was a miserable existence—but when I broke free from it, my entire life changed. Are you ready to release yourself from the shackles of the victim mentality? Keep reading to find out how.

What Is the Victim Mentality?

People with a victim mentality feel as if the world is against them and that there is a never-ending conspiracy to make their lives a living hell. Whether it's their parents, children, co-workers, or friends, they are suspicious of everyone and will often start unnecessary arguments due to paranoia. When something goes wrong, and it is clearly their fault, they won't take responsibility for their actions. Even if there is something they can do to help rectify the situation, they won't do it because they believe they are exempt from blame. Additionally, they take everything personally. They can overhear a conversation and jump to the conclusion that people talking are bad-mouthing them when the discussion has absolutely nothing to do with them. People with a victim mentality always feel resentful and think things like, "What did I ever do to deserve such an awful life?"

Childhood trauma is the root cause of a victim mentality. When children are not taught effective coping strategies at the time when the trauma occurred, it leads to the belief that life just happens to people, and they are not responsible for any of it. While this is true to a certain extent, the thought process is flawed. It is correct that you are not responsible for your trauma; regardless of the type of trauma inflicted, it was not your fault. However, healing *is* your responsibility because no one can do that for you. If it was a person who caused the traumatic event, they are not going to hold your hand through the healing process because in most cases, as far as they are concerned, they did not do anything wrong. Abusers have no empathy and have a total disregard for their victims. However, the moment you realize that *you* are the only person who can heal your wounds, life gets a lot easier.

Signs You Have a Victim Mentality

If you are not sure whether you have a victim mentality, here are some of the main signs:

Constant Blaming: Instead of accepting responsibility for where you are in life, you point the finger at everyone else. If you failed your exams, it was because you had to work part time to support yourself through college because your parents were not rich enough. If you cheated on your partner, it was because they were not giving you what you deserved so you went looking for it elsewhere.

The World Is Against Them: A person with a victim mentality believes they can't achieve anything in life because the world is against them. While it is true that life is not fair, it is also true that life is what you make it. If you believe that some mystical force is always going to stop you from achieving your goals, that is exactly what you will receive.

Can't Handle Setbacks: No one cruises through life without running into obstacles along the way. In fact, it would be fair to say that setbacks are a normal part of life. We might not like them, but we can't escape them, and so the best way to approach them is to view them as lessons. People with a victim mentality find it difficult to do this and believe that every bad situation they experience is because the world is against them.

A Negative Attitude: A person with a negative attitude has a problem for every solution. They see the bad in everything and they are miserable most of the time. As far as they are concerned, there is nothing good in the world, and people who are happy are faking it. They carry negative energy with them everywhere they go.

They Lash Out in Anger: Friends and family members feel that they've got to be very careful with what they say around people with a victim mentality because they have a tendency to lash out in anger over the slightest misunderstanding. You can't give them constructive criticism because they take it as a personal offense and get extremely angry.

They Feel Sorry for Themselves: Instead of doing what is required to get out of the situation they are in, they would rather sit around feeling sorry for themselves and lamenting over everything that has gone wrong in their lives.

They Hang Out with Complainers: As the saying goes, "Misery loves company." Victims hang around with victims and they feed off each other's negative energy. They spend the majority of their time complaining about how hard life is.

They Struggle to Make Changes: People with a victim mentality struggle to make changes because they don't believe change is possible. They are comfortable in their mess, and deep down, they are too afraid to do what is required to create the life they truly want. The fear of change is also connected to a fear of the unknown; because they can't control the outcome, they would rather remain where they are.

They Have No Confidence: They lose confidence in themselves because they have accepted the situation they are in and feel that they don't have the power to change it. They believe they are at the mercy of external factors and that there is nothing they can do to control how their life turns out.

They Don't Feel Supported: No matter how much support you give them, a person with a victim mentality doesn't feel that your support is enough. They expect everyone to rally around them and coddle them, and if they don't get that, they feel unsupported.

They Hold Grudges: If they've been offended in any way by someone, they will hold a grudge for a very long time. They expect the other person to acknowledge what they have done to them before they will even consider forgiveness. But what they don't realize is that holding a grudge hurts them more than it does the perpetrator.

They Lack Empathy: Because they are so self-absorbed, people with a victim mentality lack empathy. If a friend confides in them about something bad that has happened to them, instead of empathizing with the friend, they will cut them off to talk about how *they* once experienced something a lot worse.

They Ruminate: They spend a lot of time thinking about all the bad things that have happened to them. They turn these events over and over in their head, and get overwhelmed with emotion. One of the reasons people with a victim mentality find it so hard to let go of the past is because they are always thinking about it.

They Are Passive: People with a victim mentality just accept what life throws at them. They are not assertive and avoid taking initiative. They would rather sit back and let others do the work so that if anything goes wrong, they won't get the blame.

They Are Hyper Vigilant: They are always looking for problems and, because that is what their mind is focused on, they usually find it. Basically, they are always looking for something to confirm the narrative they have created in their head.

They Are Emotionally Unavailable: Despite the amount of complaining they do, people with a victim mentality find it difficult to express their emotions and connect on an emotional level. They display avoidant behavior when in a romantic relationship and they are reluctant to discuss their feelings.

They Believe Failure Is Permanent: When they don't get the results they were hoping for, they give up because they don't believe there is anything they can do to change their situation.

They Feel Helpless: People with a victim mentality are comfortable in their helpless state. They take the path of least resistance and allow the tides of life to carry them to their destination.

They Catastrophize: A person who catastrophizes is always thinking about the worst-case scenario. This can be triggered by something as simple as a friend not answering the phone. Instead of chalking it down to their friend being busy, and telling themselves that the friend will call back when they get a chance, they will convince themselves that their friend didn't answer the phone because they've decided that they don't like them and so they're ignoring them.

They Are Envious: Envious people want everything that everyone else has, but they are not prepared to do the work to get it. People with a victim mentality always feel as if other people's lives are better than theirs because others are lucky and life just dealt them the right cards. They are renowned for not congratulating people when they announce good news. For example, if a friend announces a job promotion, they will say something slick like, "Not everyone is as lucky as you," failing to acknowledge the blood, sweat, and tears it took for them to climb the corporate ladder.

After reading these signs, you may have come to the conclusion that you have a victim mentality. But it's not the end of the world. I used to have a victim mentality so I know it's possible to change it if you're willing to put the work in. But before I get to that, let me give you some hope by providing you examples of people who refused to accept the terrible cards they had been dealt and achieved massive success.

Successful People Who Were Raised Poor

When I had a victim mentality, I believed that all successful people were just lucky and they somehow stumbled into their fortune. I was adamant that all the rich and famous had been handpicked by some mystical force and given special privileges that lowly people like me would never have access to. But when I made the decision to change my life, and I started reading about the lives of successful people, I was shocked to find that so many of them had come from poverty-stricken backgrounds and had clawed their way to the top. The stories I read helped me transform my thinking. Here are some of them.

Oprah Winfrey: Born into a poor family in Mississippi, Oprah Winfrey was molested and abused by two family members. She ran away from home at age 13, she was pregnant at 14 and gave birth but the child died shortly after. Despite her hardships, Winfrey won a scholarship to Tennessee State University where she trained to become a journalist. The media mogul went on to host her own TV show, *The Oprah Winfrey Show*. She is currently the CEO of OWN, the Oprah Winfrey Network, and is worth an estimated $2.7 billion.

Sarah Jessica Parker: The much-loved actress, best known for her role as Carrie Bradshaw in *Sex and the City*, was raised in a family of nine. Her parents were so poor that they were unable to celebrate birthdays and holidays. There were also times when they were unable to afford to pay the phone and electricity bills. At age 11, Parker landed her first acting role. Her career took off in 1981 after moving to Hollywood to star in her first TV show, *Square Pegs*, as Patty Greene. Parker has several movies under her belt including *Honeymoon in Vegas*, *L.A. Story*, and *The Ryan White Story*. Sarah Jessica Parker is worth an estimated $200 million.

Kenny Trout: Raised by a single mother who worked as a bartender, Kenny Trout was determined to break the cycle of poverty in his family. He attended Southern Illinois University and paid for his degree by selling insurance. After graduation, he established Excel Communications, a long-distance phone company. In 1998, he sold the company for $3.5 billion.

François Pinault: François Pinault was so poor that his classmates teased him. The bullying led to him dropping out of high school to work at his family's timber trading business. He saved up every penny he earned, started buying smaller companies and flipping them for a profit. He went on to start PPR, a luxury goods company. Today, with a net worth of $39.9 billion, François Pinault is one of the richest men in France.

Leonardo DiCaprio: With box-office smashes like *The Wolf of Wall Street*, *The Revenant*, and *Titanic* to his name, no one who knew Leonardo DiCaprio during his early years could have anticipated that he would become one of the most successful actors in Hollywood. The actor says he experienced extreme poverty growing up, and witnessed a lot of violence in his poverty-stricken neighborhood. His upbringing prepared him for his role in *The Wolf of Wall Street*, which featured excessive amounts of drug use and violence.

Arnold Schwarzenegger: Best known for his role as "the Terminator," not only was Arnold Schwarzenegger raised by parents who could not afford to keep the water running or the electricity on, but his father was an alcoholic who mocked his dreams. The young Arnold was so obsessed with becoming famous that his parents believed he had mental problems and sent him to a psychiatrist. However, Schwarzenegger proved his parents wrong, moved to America and became one of the most successful actors of all time.

Celine Dion: Raised in Canada with 14 siblings, the songstress reported in an interview with CBS news that she did not have her own bedroom but slept on a bed in the corridor with three of her siblings. Her parents struggled to care for her brothers and sisters, and food and clothing were in short supply. Celine Dion started singing at the age of five, and released her first album, *The Voice of God*, in 1981. She has won six Grammys and is worth an estimated $800 million.

J.K. Rowling: The single mother who couldn't afford rent is currently worth $60 million. The author of the Harry Potter series battled with depression because her life circumstances were so hard. But while on the train to London, she got the idea to write the Harry Potter novels. Her books have sold more than 500 million copies worldwide.

Halle Berry: Raised by a single mother in Oakwood Ohio, Halle Berry wasn't born with a silver spoon in her mouth. When she set her sights on New York to become an actress, the money she had on her when she arrived in the big city quickly ran out. After her mother refused to support her financially until she found some acting work, Berry was forced to live in a homeless shelter until she got back on her feet. However, she later realized that her mother choosing not to loan her money was the best thing for her. It taught her that if she really wanted to become a successful actress, she was going to have to work extremely hard to achieve her goals because nothing was going to be handed to her on a plate.

Demi Moore: With an estimated net worth of $150 million, it's hard to believe that Demi Moore was raised in a trailer park. Her parents were alcoholics and moved around a lot. But at 16, she got tired of the instability, dropped out of high school and moved away from home. In an interview with *The Guardian*, Moore says she was poor enough to notice that she didn't have the same privileges as other children. She went into acting and gave it her all because she felt as if she had nothing to lose. The evidence suggests that her efforts paid off.

Sylvester Stallone: Known for his role as Rocky Balboa in the Rocky movies, Sylvester Stallone is a well-respected actor in

Hollywood. But life hasn't always been easy for him. Due to his parents' tumultuous relationship, he spent time in foster care. His rough upbringing led to many emotional and behavioral struggles, which resulted in him being expelled from several schools. As a struggling actor unable to find work, things got so bad for him that he spent three nights sleeping at New York's Port Authority bus terminal because he couldn't afford to pay his rent. At his lowest, he was forced to sell his dog for $25 because he didn't have enough money to feed him. Despite his humble beginnings, the actor, screenwriter, and film director is today worth $500 million.

Billy Bob Thornton: His family was so poor that going to bed hungry was the norm. Most of his meals came from the leftovers his grandfather brought home from hunting. His father was extremely abusive, and the entire family suffered at his hands. Once Thornton was old enough to get a job, he would work in factories and perform in music gigs to help pay the bills. To make matters worse, Thornton was dyslexic, and because he received no help for his condition, he didn't do very well in school. He was a pretty good baseball player and hoped to play as a professional. However, during a trial for the Kansas City Royals, he sustained an injury that took him out of the game for good. He later decided to become an actor, but was told he would never be good enough so he shouldn't waste his time. His mother was the only person who encouraged him to pursue an acting career. Today, he is a successful actor with 27 awards and 69 nominations under his belt. Billy Bob Thornton has a net worth of $45 million.

Steve Jobs: The late Steve Jobs, founder of Apple, is known as one of the most successful men of all time. When he died in

2011, he was worth an estimated $10.2 billion. However, he was raised by poor parents who struggled to keep a roof over their children's heads and put food on the table. Jobs was obsessed with computers but hated school. After the first semester, he dropped out of college and went to work for a video game production company called Atari. Shortly after, he teamed up with Steve Wozniak and created the first Apple machine. Jobs made his first million at 23 years old. Within a year, he was worth $10 million, and by the age of 25, Steve Jobs was worth $100 million.

I could go on and on with this list, but I think you get my point. If people raised in the most poverty-stricken environments can become successful, so can you. Success is available to *everyone* if you are willing to change the way you think. After reading these stories, are you ready to ditch the victim mentality?

How to Ditch the Victim Mentality

It's important to understand that it is going to take a while to overcome the victim mentality. When you start putting these principles into practice, it is going to feel unnatural. You've been thinking this way for years and it has become the norm to you, so your brain is going to struggle with this new way of thinking. This is what happens when you step outside your comfort zone: everything in you will fight to return to it. But I can promise you that if you persevere, you will overcome the victim mentality.

Educate Yourself: Understanding the victim mentality will help you tremendously on your personal development journey. It will help free you from the bondage of blame so you can reap the benefits of taking responsibility for your actions. Once you free yourself from the victim mentality, you will no longer be a passive bystander, but an active player in this game called life.

There is a lot more to the victim mentality; what you have read in this chapter is just the tip of the iceberg. Many books have been written on the subject, and it will serve you well to read them. The more you know about the problems you have, the more self-aware you will become, and the easier it will be to resolve them. It's up to you what books you read, but the three that were the most helpful for me were: *Can't Hurt Me* by David Goggins; *Guiding Principles of Life Beyond Victim Consciousness* by Lynne Forrest; and *Pulling Your Own Strings* by Wayne Dyer.

Forgive People: I was reading *A Return to Love* by Marianne Williamson and she said, "Unforgiveness is like drinking poison yourself and waiting for the other person to die." And it hit me like a ton of bricks. All the anger I held in my heart for those who had hurt me was only affecting *me*. I did some further research and discovered that unforgiveness is like a cancer; it eats away at the mind, body, and soul. A study reported by Johns Hopkins Medicine found that forgiveness lowers stress levels, anxiety, and depression; it improves blood pressure, cholesterol levels, and sleep. It also lowers the risk of heart attack. On the other hand, chronic anger keeps the body in fight-or-flight mode, which means that excess cortisol is constantly flowing through the bloodstream. Too much cortisol in the body can increase the risk of diabetes, high blood pressure, and heart disease. A person who is always angry is also more prone to depression.

With that said, the question is *How do you forgive people*? First, it's important to understand that forgiveness is not a feeling; it's a choice. Second, forgiveness does not necessarily mean you let the people who hurt you back into your life—you don't even need to *speak* to them. And finally, forgiveness does not require an apology from the perpetrator. Okay, let's break that down.

When you decide to forgive the person/people who have hurt you, you are not going to experience some life-changing feeling that lets you know forgiveness has been accomplished. As mentioned, forgiveness is a choice; it's about you making the decision to release the perpetrator from your heart and allow the universe to deal with them. It's also important to mention that forgiveness does not mean you wish for something equally bad to happen to them. When I say *allow the universe to deal with them*, I mean to bring them to a place of repentance. And yes, in one way or another, they will get their karma because whatever you put out into the world comes right back to you. You will always reap exactly what you have sown. But my point is that hurt people hurt people, and whatever they did to you wasn't because they are inherently evil, but because that's the way people who haven't dealt with their trauma act. The only way this world is going to become a better place is if everyone heals their own soul and learns to love themselves. When you love yourself, you treat others the way you want to be treated. When you decide to forgive, you set this power in motion.

Oprah Winfrey told a powerful story about forgiving her mother that really touched my heart. Her mother's name was Lee. She gave birth to Oprah at age 17. Because she needed to work, Lee gave Oprah to her mother, whom she lived with for six years. During that time, Oprah was molested and assaulted by two family members, so she ran away to live with her father. Oprah never developed a relationship with her mother; she resented her for leaving her with her grandmother and for the molestation that took place while living under the woman's roof. Oprah didn't see her mother again until she became famous and her mother attempted to come back into her life to live off her success. In an interview with NBC, when asked whether she was a good mother, Lee responded that she loved Oprah, she was the best mother in the world, and had it not been for her, Oprah would not be where she is today. Her statement infuriated Oprah, but during her time of self-reflection, she came to the conclusion that her mother was indeed correct. Her mother was raised in an abusive household and so to her, abuse was love. She gave birth at the age of 17 and knew nothing about how to raise a child. Lee did the best she could with the tools she had been given. Had Oprah not been subjected to such trauma, she would not have had the resilience to become as successful as she is today.

When Lee was on her deathbed, Oprah sat with her during her final moments and said:

> "Thank you. Thank you because I know it's been hard for you. It was hard for you as a young girl having a baby, in Mississippi. No education. No training. No skills. Seventeen, you got pregnant with this baby. Lots of people would have told you to give that baby away. Lots of people would've told you to abort that baby. You didn't do that. I know that was hard. I want you to know that no matter what, I know that you did the best you knew how to do. And look how it turned out."

Oprah Winfrey forgave her mother because she developed empathy for her. She learned to see things from her perspective, and once she did that, she was free to forgive her mother. But Oprah had to make a *choice* to forgive her mother; she knew that holding on to resentment did not benefit her. It wasn't an easy decision to make, but she did it.

Next, forgiveness does not mean you have to allow the perpetrator into your life again. While forgiveness means you have released that person and the grudge you held against them, you have the right to protect yourself from being hurt again. For example, let's say you were in a domestic violence situation and broke up with your partner—you do not need to contact your ex and tell them they are forgiven. Once a door like that has been closed, leave it closed. In fact, you don't need to call *anyone* and tell them they're forgiven; that's between you and the universe. If you don't trust the person you are forgiving, and you feel there is a possibility they might hurt you again, don't attempt to rekindle the relationship.

Finally, the person you are forgiving does not need to apologize to you. Oprah did not mention that her mother apologized for all the hurt she had caused her, and there is a possibility that she never did. Remember what Lee said in her interview; she truly believed she was responsible for Oprah's success. As far as she was concerned, she had done nothing wrong. Oprah's mother didn't have any self-awareness; she couldn't see how her actions had affected her daughter. The person who hurt you might feel the same way. Some people simply don't have the ability to think that deeply—which means that if you are waiting for the perpetrator to acknowledge what they have done to you and apologize, there is a high chance you will be waiting until the end of your days. Therefore, it's important to let go of your right to an apology because that will make you even more bitter.

Additionally, forgiveness is not a onetime event. Once you've made the decision to forgive, you will go through moments where resentment rears its ugly head and you start thinking about what the person did to you, and you get angry again. During these moments, don't suppress your feelings; acknowledge them, but don't allow them to consume you. Once you feel you are ready, forgive the person again.

Forgive Yourself: As I've mentioned, you are where you are today because of the choices you've made. This is a bitter pill to swallow, but it's the truth. The thing that stops you from taking action towards your goals are the excuses you tell yourself because you have internalized the negative labels that have been placed on you. Whether these labels came from childhood or an abusive partner, you accepted them and they became a self-fulfilling prophecy. When I realized this, I got angry at myself for being stupid enough to accept such negative labels—but I didn't know any better. And when you know better, you do better.

Oprah Winfrey went through the same thing. She spent her early life being promiscuous and giving her body away to men who didn't deserve it. It wasn't until many years later, on her personal development journey, that she realized her promiscuity was a manifestation of who she believed she was. Her childhood had taught her that she was worthless and that nobody wanted her. The molestation further solidified this belief. By sleeping with men, she thought she was getting the validation she needed. But every time a man left her after he had gotten what he wanted, she felt even more insignificant, and thus the cycle continued. Oprah had to forgive herself for internalizing those beliefs and allowing them to lead her down a path of destruction.

Meditate: Meditation is a powerful tool to help you overcome the victim mentality because it trains us to change our thinking and develop a new perspective about our circumstances. It helps us create mental space so we can build clarity. Meditation also helps you connect with yourself on a deeper level. Here is a ten-minute meditation that will help you deal with unforgiveness:

- Set an alarm for 10 minutes.
- Sit in a comfortable position with your back straight and your eyes closed.
- Start taking slow, deep breaths, in through your nose and out through your mouth.
- Observe each breath as it travels through your body.
- Think about the good things that have happened in your life and why you are grateful for them.
- To help you develop compassion, think about a person who has experienced suffering. Say to yourself, "May *[name of person]* suffer no more."
- Imagine the person saying the same thing back to you.
- Continue taking deep breaths, and form a deeper connection with the suffering person.
- Now think about people who have hurt you. This could be recent or sometime in the past.
- Forgive each person one by one, starting with the smaller transgressions.
- Think about the struggles they may have had in life and the fact that they are human just like you, which means they are susceptible to making mistakes.
- Continue breathing while focusing on your breath until the alarm goes off.

Create a Mantra: A mantra is a form of self-talk that empowers you to override negative self-talk. We all have an inner voice that speaks to us more than anyone else does. But if you don't know how to control it, that voice will convince you that all your insecurities are true and that you are the worst person in the world. When you catch yourself thinking like this, repeating a mantra will snap you out of your pity party real quick. A great way to create a mantra is to go back to your journal and read through your thoughts. Your thoughts will reveal your insecurities, and you can create a mantra that neutralizes them. Here's a mantra that works for me: "I am not a victim of my circumstances. I have the power to create the life I want."

Practice Self-Compassion: Self-compassion is essential on this difficult journey. You have chosen to change your life, and there are going to be many ups and downs along the way. Firstly, you are not going to get it right all the time, and sometimes you simply won't feel like putting in any effort—and that's okay. It takes an immense amount of self-discipline to transform your thinking and overcome a destructive habit you've engaged in for years. The victim mentality has literally become a part of your personality, and shedding it is going to take work. Self-compassion will give you the encouragement you need to keep going when you are struggling. We are our harshest critics, and we have the tendency to beat ourselves up if we are not in perfection mode at all times. But think about it like this: if a friend or family member confided in you that life wasn't treating them very kindly at the moment, what would you do? You would be kind and compassionate towards them, you would encourage them and gently remind them that everything is going to be okay. That is how you should speak to *yourself* when things are not going well. Your kind words will soothe you, calm you down, and give you a sense of peace.

Take Responsibility: One of the main components of the victim mentality is playing the blame game. Nothing is ever your fault, and you are constantly pointing the finger at everyone else. If you're late for work, it's because the traffic was terrible—but the reality is that you hit the snooze button ten times before getting out of bed. If you didn't get the promotion, it's because your manager has a vendetta against you—but the reality is that you've consistently demonstrated that you are not ready to take on more responsibility. This is what playing the blame game looks like. But taking responsibility for your actions means you accept whatever consequences life throws at you, and these can be positive or negative. People with a victim mentality have no problem taking the credit when things go well for them, but when they go wrong, that's when the finger-pointing starts. The following tips will help you take responsibility for your actions:

- **Everything Is Your Fault:** Hopper, a villain from the movie *A Bug's Life,* made the wise statement that the first rule of leadership is that everything is your fault. This rule seems pretty unfair when there are plenty of circumstances that are beyond your control that can contribute to things going wrong. However, it's also important to understand that an effective leader never places blame; they carry the responsibility for the team. Whether it's your fault or not, as a leader, you must always carry the blame.

"What has this got to do with ditching the victim mentality?" I hear you asking. The answer—everything! You must first know how to govern yourself before you can govern others. You are the leader of your life, which means it is your responsibility to manage it effectively. While there are some things in your life you have no control over, learn to accept them without making excuses and placing blame. From this moment onwards, adopt the mentality that when things go wrong in your life, it is your fault, no matter how many excuses you might be able to come up with to convince yourself otherwise.

- **Accept Your Emotions:** Taking responsibility for your actions won't feel good when you are so used to deflecting. But it's all a part of the process and something you must learn to deal with. When you experience negative emotions, analyze them and determine why you feel the way you do. Is it guilt, sadness, or shame? You might experience shame when accepting responsibility for your actions because when you really think about it, you realize that the actions that led to the negative experience were embarrassing. That's fine—accept it, move on, and do what needs to be done to ensure you don't make the same mistake twice.

- **Don't React:** The first thing most people do when facing a difficult situation is get defensive and react without thinking. They immediately go into defense mode to protect themselves from blame. But the first thing you should do is pause, take a break, and remove yourself from the situation. Once you've calmed down, you can look at it from a different perspective. You can calm yourself down by taking slow, deep breaths, going for a walk, or calling a friend to discuss the situation. Once you learn how to stop reacting to situations, your decision-making skills will improve.

The victim mentality will hold you back from everything you want in life. Therefore, it is essential that you do the work required to overcome it. I suffered from the victim mentality for most of my life, so I know how crippling it can be. Understanding why I thought this way, and learning and implementing a new way of thinking really helped me get past this difficult stage. In the next chapter, I'll give you more insight into how important your mind is in this transformative process.

CHAPTER 3:

IT STARTS IN THE MIND: THINK AND GROW RICH

*"A man is but the product of his thoughts.
What he thinks, he becomes."*
—Mahatma Gandhi

What is the most powerful weapon in the world? I always ask my audiences this question, and the most common answer I get is *the nuclear weapon*. While I understand that someone would say this because one nuclear bomb can kill millions of people, it is the wrong answer. The most powerful weapon in the world is the human mind because that is where the idea for the nuclear weapon was birthed. Everything that was ever created on this earth started in the mind. The mind is capable of imagining, and then the person who conceives the idea works to create it. Using the same principle, if you can envision yourself living the life of your dreams, you can also create it. In his book *Think and Grow Rich*, Napoleon Hill said, "Whatever your mind can conceive and believe, it can achieve." This is a bold statement, but for many, it has proven true. Let's take a look at why.

Thoughts Are Energy

The world we live in is one big ball of energy; we are surrounded by energy particles and they form together to create matter. Everything is energy, including your thoughts, words, and actions. Whatever you think about becomes your reality because the energy from your thoughts connects with the energy from your environment, and it is this process that creates your reality. The more energy you direct towards your thoughts, words, and actions, the faster you will see a manifestation.

In order to change your life, you must first understand the role you play in the energetic sphere. The question is, what type of energy are you putting into your thoughts? There are only two types of energy, high and low, and your ability to manifest depends on the level of energy you put out. Energy travels at certain speeds—the lower the energy, the slower it travels; the higher the energy, the faster it travels. Water is a substance; when its energy is low, it forms ice, and when its energy is high, it turns into vapor. Heat is high energy, and when it makes contact with ice, it will melt into water and eventually turn into vapor. The transformation only takes place when the energy is added. If your thoughts are of a low energy, to change them you'll need to add some high energy to those thoughts. But before we get into how to do that, let's take a look at why you have low-energy thoughts.

How Limiting Beliefs Are Affecting You

When I remember that only 1% of the population earns 50% of the world's wealth, I become convinced that the majority of people hold limiting beliefs about themselves. Limiting beliefs are the negative beliefs we hold about ourselves that prevent us from reaching our full potential. These beliefs are false and fear-based, and they stop us from taking opportunities that could lift us to the next level. For example, a person who holds a limiting belief that they are not good at public speaking will turn the offer down when it is presented to them because they have convinced themselves they will be a failure. A negative mindset is also a symptom of limiting beliefs. Negative thinking will destroy your mental health and hold you back from moving forwards in life. Most people are not aware that they hold limiting beliefs because they have done so all their lives. The good news is that once you recognize that you hold limiting beliefs, you can overcome them. Here are some examples of limiting beliefs:

- "I will never be able to handle this project on my own because I'm not good enough."
- "I could never become a manager because I'm too old/young."
- "I'm too busy to spend time investing in myself."
- "I'm not clever enough to host this meeting."
- "I don't have enough experience to get a better job."
- "I'll never be as successful as those people."
- "I can't enjoy life because I don't have the money."
- "I'll never be at the top of my game."
- "I'll never get a promotion because I don't have the right skills."
- "I don't have any confidence so I could never be a good leader."
- "I'm not good enough for anyone to love me."
- "I'm not attractive enough to be in a relationship."

Everyone has these fears from time to time, but the difference between those who hold limiting beliefs and those who don't is that people with limiting beliefs actually believe their negative thoughts and allow them to stop them from succeeding in life. If these thoughts resonate with you and you agree that they have stopped you from doing the things you desire, you are already on your way to overcoming your limiting beliefs. Nevertheless, before you start working on overcoming them, it's important to understand where they came from.

Family Beliefs and Values: Your family and the people you were raised with were your first teachers. Before you were even consciously aware, they were teaching you their belief and value systems. These beliefs and values were the foundation of your core beliefs. Your young mind wasn't developed enough to question what they were teaching you, so you just accepted it as facts. If you were poor, your grandmother may have continuously talked about how only certain people get rich. If your father was very industrious, he may have pushed his children to believe that hard work was the only way to succeed. A mother might encourage her daughters to ensure they only marry rich men who will give them a better life. These beliefs could be about anything, including hobbies, taste in music, or a particular career path. The point is that they were *their* beliefs and they passed them down to you.

Education: School is not the only place we receive an education. We learn from everyone, including friends, family, and work colleagues. When a person shares their beliefs, we absorb them. If you admire the person doing the teaching, you are more likely to believe what they say.

Life Experiences: Some life experiences are more memorable than others and they will influence how you respond to things in the future. For example, if you fell off your bike and broke your arm when you were five years old, the incident may have mentally scarred you so badly that as an adult, you have no desire to ride bicycles.

HOW TO RECOGNIZE LIMITING BELIEFS

Most people who have limiting beliefs don't know they have them because that way of thinking has become the norm to them, and so they don't question their beliefs. However, when you take a step back and analyze what you're thinking about, you gain clear insight into how unhealthy your mindset is. Here are some tips on how to identify your limiting beliefs:

Evaluate Your Behavior: Evaluating your behavior will help expose your limiting beliefs. When was the last time someone upset you and you needed to express your pain to that person? How did you react? Did you say what you needed to say, or did you keep your feelings to yourself? Situations like this reveal that one of the limiting beliefs you have is that you avoid conflict. Generally, people avoid conflict because they are people pleasers and don't like disrupting the status quo. By avoiding conflict they feel they are keeping the peace—when the reality is that they are making things worse.

Put Your Beliefs on Paper: What do you believe in? Get a pen and paper, find somewhere quiet where you won't be disturbed, and spend 30 minutes writing a detailed account of your beliefs. You can divide them into sections like family, relationships, health. Don't give too much thought to what you are writing—just let it flow. Once you are done, read over them and determine which ones are limiting beliefs.

Describe Your Challenges: Do you have things in your life that you find challenging, and instead of trying to work through these challenges, you avoid them? Look for patterns in these challenges because they will give you insight into your limiting beliefs.

How to Overcome Limiting Beliefs

Now you have a full understanding of limiting beliefs, overcoming them is the next step. It's important to mention that you are not going to overcome your limiting beliefs overnight. In most cases, you will have held these beliefs since childhood; therefore it is going to take a lot of work to rid yourself of them. But if you're ready... let's go!

Step 1 – Recognize the Belief: As mentioned, most people don't know they have limiting beliefs even though they act like a compass and guide all our actions. You can compare it to following invisible signs on a road. You don't know they're there, but you're still following them and you end up braking at the wrong time and taking wrong turns down roads that lead to dead ends.

One of the most interesting facts about limiting beliefs is that their purpose is to protect you. The reason we develop limiting beliefs is to protect us from disappointment and pain. However, they become a problem when they form our adult identity, despite being developed during childhood.

Earlier, I asked you to evaluate your behavior, put your beliefs on paper, and describe your challenges. Look over the things you wrote down and try and work out what your limiting beliefs are. Whatever you think they are, write them down.

Step 2 – The Beliefs' Origin: Now that you've identified your limiting beliefs, the next step is to determine their origin. Understanding the root cause of your limiting beliefs will make it easier to overcome them because you will realize how untruthful they are. A lot of our limiting beliefs are connected to childhood experiences that have no relevance to us today. On my healing journey, I discovered that one of my limiting beliefs was that I wasn't a good writer. I had spent many years writing a book; every year, I would make a New Year's resolution that I would finish the book that year, but I never did. I would start, only to stop within a few weeks and not go back to it until the following year. When I would read over what I had written, I told myself it wasn't good enough, and that no one was ever going to buy my books. When I did some digging, I realized that this limiting belief came from my fourth-grade teacher. She had asked everyone to stand up in front of the class and say what they wanted to do for a living. I remember confidently marching up to the front of the class and saying, "I want to be an author and write an entire library of books!" My teacher, Mrs. Williams, told me I should choose another profession because I wasn't a good writer. My confidence in my writing skills left me that day.

Despite the fact that I went on to complete an English degree, I had internalized Mrs. Williams' nasty comments, and deep down I didn't think I was good enough to be an author—hence the reason I kept putting off writing my book. You can also develop limiting beliefs as an adult. For example, a relationship breakdown might be so painful that you become resistant to relationships.

Spend time thinking about where your limiting beliefs came from, because once you unravel these memories, you can work on forgiving the people who hurt you, and let go of those negative experiences. It will also allow you to start working on forgiving *yourself* for allowing them to affect you the way they have. All of which will help you in finally letting go.

Step 3 – How It Has Hindered You: Once you start working on yourself, there's a high chance you'll discover you have several limiting beliefs. Another limiting belief I had was that I didn't deserve to be rich because I hadn't been handpicked by some mystical universal force. While I love my parents dearly, we lived from hand to mouth. We didn't go on vacations or get fancy presents because there was never enough money. All I heard growing up was, "Those things are for rich people and we will never be rich, so be grateful for what you've got." This was another message I internalized, and as a result, I found it extremely difficult to succeed.

Now that you've identified your limiting beliefs and you know where they came from, it's time to evaluate your life and pinpoint how your limiting beliefs have held you back. By writing down the role your limiting belief has played in harming you, your subconscious mind starts to recognize how destructive this belief is and that it is not helpful to you. Be warned that this task is difficult because it isn't easy to relive painful memories. You might start wondering what your life could have been like had you not experienced the trauma in your childhood or adult life. Nevertheless, it's essential to gain a full understanding of how damaging limiting beliefs are and how important it is to overcome them. Therefore, while you are acknowledging how your limiting beliefs have hindered you, embrace the emotions that accompany this process. There will be a lot of discomfort and pain, but that's perfectly normal. Once you release those emotions, it will be easier for you to say goodbye to your limiting beliefs.

Start by sitting in a quiet location where you won't be disturbed. Spend about five minutes taking slow, deep breaths to relax your mind and body. Write down the limiting belief at the top of the page and then, in a numbered list, write down all the ways the limiting belief has held you back. For example, if your limiting belief is that you don't deserve love, you might write down the following:

1. I have allowed men/women to treat me badly in relationships because I didn't believe I deserved love.

2. I have sabotaged perfectly good relationships because I didn't believe I deserved love.

3. I would be married with children by now if it wasn't for the limiting belief that I don't deserve love.

4. I feel terribly jealous when I see couples because I don't believe I deserve love.

Again, you are going to feel all sorts of negative emotions when you are writing out this list because you'll be reflecting on all the wasted chances and lost opportunities. However, as hard as this will be, try and see it as a positive thing because it will give you the momentum to overcome these limiting beliefs so they no longer hold you back and stop you from reaching your full potential. The next step is to challenge these beliefs.

Step 4 – Challenge the Beliefs: The most effective way to start this process is to understand that these beliefs are not facts. You may feel as if they are true, but they are not a reflection of who you truly are and your real capabilities. Limiting beliefs are a false representation of you. When I understood this revelation, it hit me like a ton of bricks—I had been living as an imposter my entire life. The insecure, scared, angry man I had become was not who I was born to be. When I discovered who I was and what I was capable of, it blew my mind. Likewise, *you* have been living as an imposter your entire life; you were born to be an unstoppable force of nature, with gifts and talents to bless the world. But unfortunately, because your parents didn't know who *they* were, they couldn't tell you who *you* were. But today, *I* am telling you who you are—and it's not who you think you are at the moment.

Changing your limiting beliefs is going to be a fight; your subconscious mind is going to challenge you to remain who you are because that's who it's programmed you to be. It's a constant uphill battle—you'll find you have a couple of good days where your mind is strong and you are prepared to conquer the world, but all of a sudden, you'll fall back into old habits and will feel as if you're back at first base. The key is perseverance. No matter how many times you fall, get back up.

Limiting beliefs lose their power once you realize they are not true, so question yourself. Whatever your limiting beliefs are, interrogate them. Where is the evidence that you can't become an author because you have no writing skills? Where is the evidence that no one will ever love you because you are not good enough? Where is the evidence that you'll never own your own business because you're not smart enough? Now, because you've held these limiting beliefs for most of your life, you're going to come up with plenty of REASONS that confirm these beliefs. However, reasons are not FACTS. In a court of law, the evidence presented must be factual before a person is found guilty. A lawyer can't put a witness on the stand who *thinks* they saw the gunman walking out of the apartment that the crime took place in. That evidence is not strong enough, and it is unlikely to convince a jury to find the accused guilty. However, if the lawyer plays a video tape of the accused walking out of the apartment where the crime took place, he can't deny it. I have said all that to say this: the evidence that you have against yourself is weak, and you can test that evidence by achieving your dreams.

Now I want you to get a pen and paper and write down what your world would look like if you didn't hold these limiting beliefs. What if you were wrong? Challenge yourself to start envisioning your ideal world as a confident, bold individual who achieves anything they set their mind to. The next thing I want you to do is write down all the ways you can prove that these beliefs are wrong. For example, as you know, one of my limiting beliefs was that I had terrible writing skills. However, I managed to get high grades in all my essays, and I got the top mark in my degree. In fact, I won an award for the best dissertation of the year! That is strong evidence that I am a good writer and proves that my limiting belief was false. What strong evidence do you have that proves your limiting belief was false?

This activity is not a "one and done." You might go to bed feeling a bit better, but when you wake up in the morning, your negative thinking will attack your mind. When this happens, it's time to put on your armor (everything you've learned in this chapter) and fight back. Meditate on what your world would look like if you didn't have any limiting beliefs, and remind yourself of the evidence that refutes those beliefs.

Step 5 – Choose a New Belief: Armed with a vision of your ideal world, you can create a new belief. The key to conquering limiting beliefs is to change them into something you can believe. Basically, it should be realistic. It's a bad idea to jump from "I am a terrible writer" to "I am going to become a *New York Times* bestseller." While this is an awesome long-term goal to have, starting small makes it easier to change the belief. I went from believing "I am a terrible writer" to "I am capable of writing a book." To reprogram my mind, every morning and every evening, I wrote out, "I am capable of writing a book" ten times. And then I took action by writing 500 words of the book per day, and within six months, I had written the book. I was able to achieve this for two reasons: one, because the goal was realistic; and two, because I focused on the goal and not the obstacles. Before, I had focused on the obstacles, and it was more than not believing that I was a good writer—I had many excuses, such as, "I won't be able to find a publisher; I don't have enough time; no one is going to be interested in reading the type of books I write—so why bother?" The more I focused on these excuses, the less motivated I became to write the book. Motivational speaker Simon Sinek spoke about how skiers are capable of skiing through trees. To the people watching, it looks extremely difficult because all they can see are the trees. However, the skiers are trained not to focus on the trees (obstacles), but the path of snow that will lead them to their destination. Use the same principle: don't focus on the obstacles, because there will be many—instead, focus on the path that will lead to your destination.

When I started writing my new beliefs down, I didn't believe them; in fact, I felt as if I was lying to myself. But instead of putting the pen down and giving up, I continued, despite how I felt. I took the activity up as a 30-day challenge. I got a large sheet of paper, titled it, "30-Day Challenge to Change Limiting Belief and Take Action." I then wrote the numbers 1–30 on the paper and stuck it on my wall right above my light switch to make sure I saw it every day. The challenge involved writing out my new belief 10 times every morning and night, and writing 500 words of my book. I didn't feel confident at the beginning; however, I noticed that my confidence grew each time I crossed off a day. By the end of the 30 days, I had written 15,000 words of my book! That was more than I had written in the entire seven years I had been trying to write it. The target word count for the book was 100,000 words. I knew that if I continued writing for another six months, I could finish the book, and that's exactly what I did. Every month, I felt my confidence grow, and when I had completed the book, I began a new chapter in my life. I wasn't the same person anymore; the old me had died. I was now a new creation, the person I was destined to be.

I know you can do it too. All it takes is 30 days to build momentum, and once you get going, you won't be able to stop. Get a sheet of paper, and at the top of it, write, "30-Day Challenge to Change Limiting Belief and Take Action." Write out the numbers 1–30, stick the piece of paper somewhere you know you are going to see it every day. I stuck mine over the light switch in my bedroom, but you can stick it anywhere, such as on your fridge, mirror, or front door. Each day you complete the challenge, cross out a number. However, if you fail to do it on one day, you'll need to start again from number one. The key to changing your mindset is consistency, and this is most important at the beginning of your journey.

Step 6 – Take Your Power Back: As discussed, you didn't give yourself limiting beliefs—they were given to you. When you realize this, it's easy to start pointing fingers and blaming others for the position you are currently in. When I remembered what my teacher had said to me, and realized her words were the reason I was stuck in life, I hated her with a passion. But it also gave me even more of an excuse not to write the book because I had someone to blame for not writing it. Essentially, this woman had stolen my destiny with her words, but it was my job to take it back. No one else could do that but me. By me accepting that I wasn't good enough to become an author, she had power over me. Those were *her* words and not mine. At the time, I was this confident little kid who fully believed I would become an author. But the moment her words touched my ears, I stopped believing it. And the more I thought about what she said, the more I believed it was true. When I wrote my first book, I took my power back. Now it's your turn.

The people who gave you your limiting beliefs have hijacked your destiny. They are in possession of something that doesn't belong to them. TAKE IT BACK! The way you take it back is by refusing to believe it and achieving the very thing they convinced you was impossible to achieve. Listen; life is not a bed of roses—you've got to fight for what belongs to you. This is not a physical fight but a mental fight; remember, your mind is the most powerful weapon in the world. However, it can either work for or against you. The choice is yours. There is something you have been created to do on this earth, and that space has been reserved solely for you. Whether you leave this world having achieved your assignment and made the impact you were supposed to make is up to you. So, let's get this show on the road and take your power back!

Step 7 ~ Practice Self-Compassion: This journey is a difficult one. In fact, I'll be so bold as to say it's the most difficult thing you're ever going to do. But it has to be done if you're going achieve anything in life. Think about it like this: the foundation of your home is the most important part of the building. However, when someone sees a beautiful home, the foundation doesn't cross their mind—all they're focused on is how beautiful it is. Additionally, a lot of people think the most important part of their house is the roof because it protects them from elements such as wind, rain, and snow. While it is true that the roof is important, it's not as important as the foundation.

The foundation bears the weight of your home and completely supports it. With an unstable base, it won't be long before the structure starts to collapse. Therefore, construction workers put more time and energy into building the foundation of a home than any other part of the building. Here are some reasons the foundation is the most important part of your home:

It Supports Your Home: The foundation is underneath the ground of your home. Its main purpose is to keep your house standing. If your house had no foundation, it would quickly collapse into the ground, which would cause a great deal of damage to your home. However, a well-built foundation will support the home and keep it stable, regardless of the weather. But building a strong foundation requires a lot more than just pouring concrete into a hole in the ground. A lot of work goes into the process, from finding the right materials to taking into consideration the soil and the geology. The foundation must be strong enough to support the weight of your home even when there are changes to the ground beneath it.

It Prevents Movement: Natural forces don't sleep; they are always working. The temperature changes, the soil's moisture levels fluctuate, and so many other things. If your home is not properly anchored to the foundation, the natural forces will destroy it. A strong foundation will not succumb to any movement caused by natural forces.

It Insulates Your Home: The foundation also keeps your house warm, even during the coldest temperatures, which will save you a lot of money during the winter months.

It Keeps Water Out: Moisture causes a lot of damage to buildings. When water from the rain and snow settles around your house, it soaks into the soil. Plant and tree roots can also add to the water surrounding your house. This causes the soil to shift and expand, which puts pressure on the foundation. A strong foundation and good drainage will keep your house dry no matter how bad the weather is.

Once a strong foundation has been built, it is then time to build the structure of the house—you know, the fancy part that everyone admires. "So what has this got to do with self-compassion?" I hear you say. Firstly, your mind is the foundation of your destiny; if it isn't strong, you won't be able to carry the weight of what you have been called to do. Becoming successful is a huge responsibility, and there will be a heavy load on your shoulders. It requires perseverance and self-discipline. Without these, you won't succeed. As mentioned, the journey isn't going to be an easy one; there will be many obstacles along the way. And without a strong mind, you'll give up at the first sign of trouble. By strengthening your mind before you start working on achieving your goals, the storms of life will not be able to derail you. Secondly, because the foundation is the hardest part to build, it takes a while to build it. Construction workers are often forced to start over many times before they get it right. Likewise, you are not going to get it right immediately. You are not going to become a pillar of strength within a few weeks of working on your mind. You are going to keep slipping back into old habits. But as long as you keep working at it, you'll get there in the end.

When you do slip up, don't beat yourself up about it. Be kind to yourself. Remind yourself that the journey is hard and it's okay if you struggle. Change doesn't happen without a fight. Your mind will play tricks on you; it will attempt to convince you that you're wasting your time and there's no point in trying. Because it's so hard, you will want to give up, but giving up is the easiest thing to do. The majority of people give up when the going gets tough. If you were to ask one hundred people what their dreams were, whether they had achieved them, and why they hadn't achieved them, the majority would tell you they hadn't achieved their dreams, and they would give you a host of reasons for this. Most of those reasons would consist of excuses such as, "I couldn't afford it," "I started a family and I didn't have time anymore," or, "No one supported me, so I didn't feel motivated to continue." What they really mean is that they gave up because things got too hard. But if they understood that failure was a necessary part of success—I would be so bold as to say that this is a universal law—they would never give up. Napoleon Hill said:

> *"Before success comes in any man's life, he is sure to meet with much temporary defeat, and perhaps, some failure. When defeat overtakes a man, the easiest and most logical thing to do is quit. That is exactly what the majority of men do. More than 500 of the most successful men this country has ever known told the author their greatest success came just one step beyond the point at which defeat had overtaken them."*

Don't be the majority; fight the good fight of faith and keep it moving. But while you're doing it, be kind to yourself when you fall.

How to Think and Grow Rich

Before I get started, I would like to stress that I am in no way suggesting that you are going to get rich by just thinking about it. That's not how it works. Becoming successful is going to take everything you've got. Through blood, sweat, and tears, will you emerge the champion of your life. However, it takes a certain mindset to win in life. Success is nothing more than a mentality—it's about how you *think* first. The bottom line is that if you don't think you can become successful, you won't. There is a strategy to it, and in this section, I'm going going to teach you what it is.

Identify Negative Thinking: According to psychologist Rick Hanson, negativity in humans is natural because that's how the brain is hardwired. We operate from a negativity bias because when our ancestors lived in caves, thinking the worst kept their brains alert so they were always ready in the event that danger presented itself. Thousands of years ago, this is what kept people alive; they were so focused on dangers and threats that they were always on the lookout for lions, bears, and tigers. However, today, things are a lot different—we are no longer surrounded by lions, bears, and tigers because there are very few of these animals left. The ones that *are* around are for the most part confined, and are not free to roam the streets. It is no longer necessary for us to think that way—yet we still do. The problem with this way of thinking is that it makes success impossible.

Positivity is an essential component of success. Tom Corley and Michael Yardney, authors of *Rich Habits, Poor Habits: Learn the Daily Habits That Separate the Rich from the Poor* named positivity as one of the most common habits of self-made millionaires. The authors studied the habits of self-made millionaires for five years and found that 79% of rich people were certain they would become rich before they did so. More than half the participants (54%) believed that optimism fueled their success. Seventy-one percent developed a habit of gratitude. Many other studies add to the validity of these findings. In 1998, psychologist Barbara Lee Fredrickson conducted a study that found positivity boosts focus, risk tolerance, and cognitive ability. All of the self-made millionaires in Corley and Yardney's book possessed these traits. Negativity hinders success for several reasons. Here are some of them:

- Decision-making and focusing on solutions instead of problems takes place in a part of the brain called the prefrontal cortex. The prefrontal cortex does not work to its full capacity when the mind is full of negativity.

- Chronic stress causes inflammation in the body, and research suggests that inflammation is responsible for conditions such as irritable bowel disease, cardiovascular disease, and cancer. Health is wealth, and when it is under attack, it is difficult to focus on normal everyday tasks, let alone on trying to achieve your goals. When you're always thinking the worst, it causes chronic stress.

- As the saying goes, "No man is an island"—in other words, you are not going to become successful on your own; you will need people to pull you up. However, pessimism and optimism don't mix, and one thing that successful people are careful about is the company they keep. Since they know positivity plays such an important role in success, they avoid negativity like the plague. Negative people are quickly rooted out of the social circles of the successful, who will warn their peers and friends to avoid them too. Basically, negativity will make you miss opportunities.

The first step on your journey to positivity is to identify negative thinking patterns. Here are some of the most common:

Polarizing: Also known as "all or nothing thinking," polarizing is when you don't have a gray area—everything is either black or white.

Perfectionism: Perfectionism is deceptive because on the surface it seems like a positive trait. However, perfectionism is rooted in fear; you desire perfection so people won't criticize you. Additionally, perfectionism causes procrastination. When you are fearful that whatever you do isn't going to be good enough, you keep putting it off.

Magnifying: You turn everything into a big deal even if it isn't. For example, the server at the McDonald's drive-through forgot to put your fries in the bag. You go into the store and explain to the server that because they forgot your fries you are going to be late for work—despite the fact that it literally took five seconds to hand you your fries!

Blaming Yourself: You give yourself these impossible tasks, like putting ten items on your to-do list. When you don't get them done, you blame yourself.

Blaming Others: You refuse to take responsibility for your actions and blame everyone else for the negative circumstances you often find yourself in.

Catastrophizing: Catastrophizing is when you always think the worst even if you have no facts to confirm what you're thinking. You slip down the stairs on your way into the kitchen to have breakfast, so you jump to the conclusion that since your day started off badly, the rest of your day will be bad too.

Personalizing: When something bad happens, you immediately blame yourself. Let's say you had planned to go out with friends, but the plans get canceled because too many people can't make it. Instead of taking it with a pinch of salt, you convince yourself that the plans were canceled because your friends don't really like you and they didn't want to hang out with you.

Filtering: You filter out the positive aspects of a situation, and magnify the negative ones. For example, you visit your sister and have a fantastic time. But at the end of the evening, she says something you don't like and you have a small disagreement. You settle the argument, and you leave on good terms. But on the way home, all you can think about is the argument, and you spend the rest of the evening thinking about it. You even call your friend to complain about it. Amidst all this complaining, you forget about the awesome time you both had.

Now that you've identified your negative thinking patterns, it's time to change them and learn to become more positive.

Practice Gratitude: Gratitude is a powerful tool to keep in your positivity arsenal. It is the practice of focusing on the good things in your life instead of focusing on the things you want but don't have. Research suggests there are many positive mental and physical benefits associated with gratitude, including less likelihood of suffering from depression and mental health issues overall. It also boosts immunity and improves heart health. Make gratitude a daily habit by doing the following:

- Decide on a time to practice gratitude and stick to it. You can do it first thing in the morning, or before going to bed.

- Use a notebook specifically dedicated to gratitude.

- Find a quiet location where you won't be disturbed.

- Sit comfortably and take deep breaths until you feel yourself relax.

- Think about three things in your life that you are grateful for. It could be anything, such as the food you have in your fridge, getting to see a friend you haven't seen in a long time, or the roses you smelled on your way home from work the other day.

- Write down the things you are grateful for.

- Once you put your pen down, think about the things you just wrote, induce the emotion of gratitude, and sit with it for a few minutes. Think about all the reasons you are grateful for these things.

Positive Self-Talk: One of the reasons I believe the world is in such a terrible state is because people don't love themselves. When you love yourself, you treat others the way you treat yourself. But if you hate yourself, you are going to treat people in the same hateful manner you treat yourself. It's that simple.

So, apply the same principle to positive self-talk. I mentioned earlier that we all have an inner voice. I sometimes wonder what the world would be like if everyone was telepathic. One thing I do know is that people would make more of an effort to control their thoughts. When I was at the height of my insecurity, I would have been embarrassed if any of my friends could read my mind and see the hateful things I used to say to myself. I was literally emotionally abusing myself. Negative self-talk is emotional abuse. You would never speak to your friends and loved ones the way you speak to yourself. Imagine saying to your best friend, "You're completely useless," "You will never amount to anything," or, "You are wasting your time setting those goals because you are never going to achieve them." You would never say such things to them—so why say them to yourself? You want your friend to win at life, so you're going to hype them up at every chance you get. That's what positive self-talk is all about—hyping yourself up every chance you get.

Positive self-talk is a habit you should incorporate into your daily routine. Continue it throughout the day, especially when you start having negative thoughts. You can engage in positive self-talk by reciting affirmations. Say them in the morning, write them down on note cards and carry them with you when you leave the house so you can repeat them during the day. Here are some positive affirmations to get you started:

- I am an overcomer, and I defeat any challenges that come my way.

- I have a limitless amount of potential and I will achieve anything I put my mind to.

- Every day I wake up, I am a better person than I was the night before.

- I radiate love, and everyone around me is positively affected by my love.

- I am strong and resilient; whatever comes my way, I can handle it.

- I am living an abundant life because I think positive things about myself.

- I deserve success and all the good things that come with it.

- I attract miracles because I am such a positive person.

- Today, I choose love, peace, and joy.

- I am so confident that everyone around me feels confident too.

- I have many abilities and talents. I trust in them and put them to good use.

- My past no longer affects me; the thought of what's coming next in my life excites me.

- My life is filled with good things because I radiate positivity and attract them into my life.

- I radiate light, and everyone benefits from my positivity.

- I am a positive person because I am in control of my mind and choose to think positive thoughts.

- I am surrounded by uplifting and positive people who believe in me.

- I have the power to turn my dreams into reality.

- I embrace challenges because I view them as opportunities for growth.

- I am a giver of love, and my heart is open to receiving love.

- I am grateful that my life is overflowing with abundance and that I will attract even more of it.

Positive Thinking: As mentioned, the mind is the most powerful weapon in the world when it is used in the right way. The most productive use of your thinking time is positive thinking. This means that your mind is continuously saturated with positive thoughts. When you experience a challenge, instead of thinking about the worst possible outcome, think about the best possible outcome and the lessons you can learn from the challenge. If you don't like someone, such as a work colleague or a friend of a friend, instead of thinking about all the reasons you don't like them, focus on their positive characteristics, even if it's that they have a nice smile, or they dress well. This doesn't mean you're being fake; it means you are choosing to see the good in them because you understand that human nature is a combination of good and bad. Everyone has something good about them, even if it's just one thing.

Additionally, use the positive affirmations above to meditate as you go about your day. Meditation isn't just about sitting in the lotus position and emptying your mind. You can also meditate by continuously thinking about something. Worrying is a form of meditation; when you are worried about something, you have sleepless nights thinking about it and it's on your mind constantly. Worrying is a form of negative thinking, though, and you can override it with positive thinking. For example, let's say you are worried about an important exam you need to pass in order to climb the career ladder. There are several reasons you are worried about the exam, including the fact you don't feel you are familiar enough with the information. There is not a lot of time left for you to learn what you need to. Or, you are not used to taking exams and you're afraid you will panic on the day. While these are legitimate concerns, it is important to understand that worrying is a pointless endeavor. Worrying doesn't serve a purpose, and it is not going to improve your situation. Worrying about future events is a waste of energy because you can't control what is going to happen. But what you *can* do is focus on the present moment by doing the following:

- **Study for the Exam:** The only thing you can do at the moment is study for the exam to the best of your ability. Give it everything you've got so that if you don't get the results you hoped for, at least your conscience is clear because you know you tried your best.

- **Let Go:** Let go of the things you can't control. If there is one thing you can't control, it's the grades you are going to get. As mentioned, in this situation, the only thing you can do is study for the exam. Whatever else happens, happens, and there is not much you can do about it.

- **Write Your Worries Down:** Get the worries out of your head and down on paper. Write down each concern, and then next to each one, write down the worst that can happen. Finally, write down why it matters if the worst happens. As you go through this process, you'll quickly realize that worrying is a waste of time.

- **Acceptance:** As the saying goes, "Hope for the best and prepare for the worst." You keep a positive mindset by hoping for the best outcome but accepting that the worst could also happen. Embracing failure is essential if you are going to succeed in life—remember, every successful person failed before they had their breakthrough moment.

Become a Giver: We live in an individualistic society where it's every man for himself. In general, people are selfish and are not concerned about anyone other than themselves and their immediate family. I believe we were born to give back to the world. We came to this earth full of the ability to give, but society has taught us that we should hoard our resources, and that the only time we should give is when we're getting something in return. That's one of the reasons some people hate volunteering—they are giving their time away for free. However, giving is one of the most rewarding things you can do. Here's why:

- **Satisfaction with Life:** One survey found that 74% of people who responded that they were very generous were more satisfied with their lives, in comparison to the participants who responded that they were not generous. They were satisfied with all aspects of their lives including friends, family, finances, and romance.

  "If you want happiness for an hour, take a nap. If you want happiness for a day, go fishing. If you want happiness for a year, inherit a fortune. If you want happiness for a lifetime, help somebody."
  —Chinese Proverb.

The greatest philosophers and thinkers throughout history all came to the same conclusion:

> *"For it is in giving that we receive."*
> —Saint Francis of Assisi
>
> *"The sole meaning of life is to serve humanity."*
> —Leo Tolstoy
>
> *"We make a living by what we get;
> we make a life by what we give."*
> —Winston Churchill
>
> *"Making money is a happiness;
> making other people happy is a superhappiness."*
> —Muhammad Yunus
>
> *"Giving back is as good for you as it is for those you are helping, because giving gives you purpose. When you have a purpose-driven life, you're a happier person."*
> —Goldie Hawn

The next time you see someone do something nice for another person, pay attention to the reaction of the giver. They light up. This reaction has been termed "giver's glow." A study conducted at Stony Brook University found that generosity releases feel-good hormones such as dopamine and serotonin. These hormones make us feel peaceful and joyful, hence the glow.

- **Better Relationships:** Givers have better relationships in general because they pour into people. They invest their time, resources, and everything else they have to offer in their relationships. Givers don't do things halfheartedly; they go all out for their loved ones, and people appreciate this, which is why they have stronger relationships.

- **Job Satisfaction:** Givers are more satisfied with their jobs because they find purpose in them. Even if it's a dead-end job they're just working at to make some extra cash, they will do more than they're supposed to and find a way to give. They never sit at their desks clock-watching, waiting for 5:00 p.m. so they can go home. Givers believe that whatever you do, you should do it to the best of your ability, even if you don't like the thing you are doing. Why? Because it helps you expand your mind and develop a growth mindset, and it's how you live with integrity.

- **A Positive Outlook:** When you are a giver, you believe that life has meaning and that you're not just roaming aimlessly through it. When you believe that life has meaning, you are not as pessimistic and have a more positive outlook.

- **Healthier:** Because generous people have a more positive outlook on life and are happier, they have better physical and mental health. They are less likely to experience negative emotions such as anxiety, apathy, depression, and hopelessness. Additionally, they are physically healthier because they don't have so much cortisol (the stress hormone) running through their body. Generous people are also more likely to exercise and consume a healthy diet.

- **Content:** Everyone experiences envy and wants things they can't have, whether it's a bigger home, a nice car, or the ideal romantic relationship. However, generous people are less likely to experience envy all the time. Givers are satisfied with what they already have, which is why it is easier for them to give. On the other hand, people who hoard their resources do so because they're not content with what they have and want to accumulate more.

- **High Self-Esteem:** Evidence suggests that generosity is good for your self-esteem. Giving makes you feel better about yourself because of the joy experienced when you give.

Focus on the Present: Being present is about paying attention to what's going on at that moment. It can mean noticing your partner looks distressed during a conversation even though they haven't told you there is anything wrong. You might feel the subtle shift in energy when someone walks into a room. Being present can mean admiring the beauty of the sunset as you're driving down the coast. However, for the average person, the mind is continuously wandering, wavering between the past, the present, and the future. Most people don't know how to be present. You could be having an important conversation with a friend but thinking about what you're going to eat for dinner. Or, while your partner is telling you about their day, your focus is on how you're going to climb the career ladder. When you are not present, whoever you are speaking to can tell.

You might have sleepless nights about a job interview you had, or the argument you had with your mother a few days ago. Your mind is like a video recorder that won't stop pressing rewind and replaying all the different scenarios you've been in. These constant thoughts prevent you from being present, which means you are never fully rested. They can also have a negative effect on your performance and relationships. It's not easy to be present, and it's very difficult to learn. Being present requires a lot of self-discipline and you must have the ability to control your mind. However, being able to disregard these ruminations and bring your full attention to the present moment has many benefits. Let's begin by learning about the importance of being in the present moment.

Each day, your body takes you through a specific routine. You wake up, go to work, and take care of your responsibilities. All of these things happen on autopilot; you don't think about it—you just do it. Being present is often confused with being *physically* present, but it has nothing to do with being present physically, and everything to do with being present mentally. It's also important to understand that we can't be present all the time; it's normal to spend some time in the past, and some in the future. But it's not normal to live there permanently. In everything you do, your mind should be right there with you. But for most people, their mind and body are often in two different places. Maybe your mind wanders when you're stressed, anxious, or bored. You could be having lunch with your partner while your mind is at home thinking about all the housework you need to do. There are several benefits associated with living in the present. Here are some of them:

- **A Better Listener:** Most people listen but don't hear because their mind is elsewhere. It's assumed that listening is easy; however, it is a skill that must be practiced in order to master it. We are constantly bombarded with distractions, so much so that it's rare to have a conversation with a friend without them looking at their phone.

To form true connections, deep listening is essential, but it has become a lost art. Communication involves more than just talking; it's an exchange between two people filled with unspoken cues and nuances. Being a good communicator isn't just about your ability to speak well. It's also about tuning into what the person is saying, and connecting with their emotions so you *truly* hear them.

To be an effective communicator, you must master the art of listening. It's about understanding body language, making eye contact, and not just listening to what's coming out of the speaker's mouth. Improving your communication skills also makes it easier for you to connect with your inner voice. One way to become a better listener is to be present. You can achieve this by turning off the TV, radio, your phone, and anything else that would cause distractions. But most importantly, connect with your *mind*. If you notice your thoughts wandering, bring them back to the conversation.

- **You'll Be Happier:** When you let go of the past, stop worrying about the future, and appreciate the present moment, your life becomes more fulfilling. Research suggests that people are happier when they spend more time living in the present. One of the many reasons for this is that being present allows you to connect with your friends and loved ones on a deeper level. When you have a strong emotional connection with people, it strengthens your relationships, which can make you happier.

- **You'll Worry Less:** Worrying involves focusing on the future and imagining scenarios that have yet to take place. Since you can't predict the future, there is no point in worrying about it, but what you *can* do is prepare for it. When you spend more time in the present moment, you worry less because your mind is not so focused on the future.

- **You'll Be More Self-Aware:** Self-awareness boosts our mental, emotional, and physical health, and positively impacts how we interact with our environment and the people around us. Having a deeper understanding of how we feel, think, and act can help us overcome the issues that are preventing us from reaching our full potential. Being present helps us become more self-aware. By keeping our attention on the *now* instead of being stuck in the past or worrying about the future, we focus more on what's taking place internally at that present moment in time. It allows us to focus on our emotions and inner voice, which enables us to accept that we are in full control of our thoughts, surrender to our emotions, and become more accepting of how things are at the moment without placing judgment on the experience or becoming attached to it.

How to Become More Present: Becoming more present in life takes practice. Here are some tips:

- **Breathe:** Breathing exercises are a great way to bring your attention to the present moment. While taking slow, deep breaths, focus on your breathing instead of on the distractions. If you find that you struggle with focusing on your breath, there are a lot of good apps that will guide you through breathing exercises.

- **Meditate:** Meditation helps your mind and body reconnect. It serves as a bridge between our emotional response to past events and the emotions attached to anticipating the future. Meditation teaches us that our focus on the past and the future has an effect on our present. Here is a quick 10-minute meditation you can incorporate into your daily routine:
  - Set an alarm clock for 10 minutes.
  - Find a location where you won't be disturbed.
  - Sit in a comfortable position with your back straight.
  - Close your eyes and take a deep breath through your nose. Feel the breath fill your lungs. While you breathe out slowly, imagine you are releasing distractions and tension. Keep breathing for a few minutes.
  - Now pay attention to your body. Start from your toes and move your way up to your head. Pay attention to any sensations you feel. If you experience any discomfort, breathe into it and release the tension as you breathe out.
  - Focus on your breath again. Pay attention to how you breathe, its natural rhythm, and how it feels as it enters and leaves your body.
  - Your mind will wander while you meditate. When you notice that your mind has gone elsewhere, focus on your breath again.
  - As you come to the end of your meditation, wiggle your toes and fingers and slowly start becoming aware of your surroundings again.
  - Open your eyes and spend a couple of minutes appreciating the present moment.

- **Ditch Social Media:** Social media helps you stay connected with friends and family, and keep up to date with what's going on around the world. However, it can also be extremely distracting. When you spend too much time scrolling, you can't focus on the present moment because you are focused on staring at a screen and more concerned about what's going on in other people's lives, as opposed to what's going on in your own. Cutting down on your social media time will give you the opportunity to spend more time in the present.

- **Acceptance:** Worrying about the future and regretting the past is a waste of energy. When you realize that you can't control what's going to happen in the future, and that you can't change the past, it becomes easier to surrender to the present. By surrendering to the present, you accept your now and stop focusing on the things you have no control over.

Practice Laughter: Have you ever paid attention to how awesome you feel after having a good laugh? That's because when we laugh, the brain releases feel-good hormones such as dopamine and serotonin. Additionally, there are several physical and mental health benefits associated with laughter, such as:

- **Improves Mood:** Depression, anxiety, and stress are all reduced when we laugh because of the release of feel-good hormones such as dopamine and serotonin.

- **Pain Relief:** The body has its own natural pain killers called endorphins, which are one of the many hormones that are released when we laugh.

- **Boosts the Immune System:** As mentioned, negative thoughts trigger the release of the stress hormone cortisol, which can cause sickness. On the other hand, positive thoughts that encourage laughter boost the immune system because they trigger the release of neuropeptides, which strengthen the immune system.

- **Releases Tension:** Laughter causes the muscles to relax and blood to circulate around the body. This helps to reduce some of the physical symptoms associated with stress.

- **Reduces Stress:** Laughter makes you feel more relaxed and reduces stress because it speeds up and then slows down the stress response, which induces a relaxed feeling.

Practicing laughter is a great way to develop a positive mindset. The good news is that you can practice laughter daily in the comfort of your home. Here's how:

- **Think of Something Funny:** Have you ever been at home alone, thought of something funny and just burst out laughing? It's not even something you mean to do—it just happens—but you end up laughing so hard you can't stop. If you think back, you'll find there are plenty of things that have made you laugh. Bring them back to memory and allow them to tickle you again.

- **Make Laughing Sounds:** By making laughing sounds, you can trick your body into laughing. Make sounds such as, "ha ha ha" or "huh huh huh." Place your hand over your stomach and pull it in while you make these sounds. Repeat these sounds faster and faster until it sounds like you are actually laughing. The sound of laughter will make you laugh for real.

- **Watch a Comedy:** Do you have any favorite comedy shows that make you laugh? Watch them again and experience the joy of laughter.

- **Lion Laughter:** Lion laughter is an exercise from laughter yoga. Here's how to do it:
  - Sit or stand in a comfortable position with your feet shoulder-width apart.
  - Take a long, deep breath through your nose and fill your lungs with air.
  - As you exhale, stick your tongue out as far as possible at the same time as opening your eyes really wide. Make the sound of a lion by roaring really loudly.
  - This is a playful exercise, so let go of any inhibitions and embrace it.
  - Take another deep breath and repeat until you release natural laughter.

- **Crying Laughter:** Crying laughter is another form of laughter yoga. Here's how to do it:
  - Sit or stand in a comfortable position with your feet shoulder-width apart.
  - Take a long, deep breath through your nose, getting plenty of air into your lungs.
  - Breathe out slowly at the same time as fake-crying.

- Make facial expressions that show you are fake-crying.
- After fake-crying for about 60 seconds, start fake-laughing.
- Alternate between fake-crying and fake-laughing until you really do start laughing.

Avoid Toxic Positivity: As you've read, there are many benefits associated with being positive. However, positivity doesn't mean that you ignore the reality of your situation. Toxic positivity involves feeling pressured to only display positive emotions and to suppress negative ones. It's highly unrealistic to be positive all the time because experiencing the full range of emotions is a normal part of life. When you are expected to only display happiness and joy when you're in a bad situation, it can cause isolation, trauma, and unhealthy coping mechanisms.

I first encountered toxic positivity at my former place of employment. My manager used to say, "Never show pain, fear, hurt, or doubt." And there were signs all over the place saying "No-Complaining Zone" or "Positive Vibes Only." The environment was extremely fake; everyone was extremely bubbly and walked around with a massive grin on their face all the time because if you were caught not smiling, someone would say, "Chin up," "Stay positive," or, "Smile—it can't be that bad." It was so annoying. You have no idea how grateful I am not to be there anymore.

Despite the growing focus on mental health issues, we are constantly bombarded with positivity messages. In a world filled with negativity, positivity messages can be beneficial. However, when we feel pressured into only expressing our positive emotions, positivity becomes destructive. Here's how toxic positivity can have a negative impact on you:

- **Affects Mental Health:** Emotions are designed to be released. When they are suppressed, it has a negative effect on your mental health. Toxic positivity can cause you to disassociate from your negative feelings. However, no matter how disconnected you feel from your negative feelings, they will eventually manifest as depression, anxiety, or some other mental health condition.

- **Prevents Connection:** You'll never experience the full richness of a relationship if you are hiding parts of yourself. Connections are formed when people are authentic, but if you pretend to be happy all the time, the people you come into contact with will ride off your energy and feel as if they too have to be happy all the time. When two people are hiding who they truly are, it's impossible to develop a meaningful connection.

- **Encourages Shame:** When people feel as if they've got to wear a mask to hide difficult or painful emotions, it implies that there is something wrong with our true feelings. This leads to feelings of guilt and shame, which makes their situation even more difficult.

- **Destroys Confidence:** When you're surrounded by people who make you feel uncomfortable for having negative emotions, it makes you feel incapable of handling the storms of life. Whether directly or indirectly, when you're constantly told that you're not strong enough, it destroys your confidence.

- **Increases Stress:** Ignoring your emotions increases your stress levels. One study involved two groups of participants watching an emotional film while having their heart rates monitored. One group was told to express their emotions; the other group was told to hide their emotions. The results showed that those who hid their emotions had a much higher heart rate.

It's a wonderful thing that you want to embark on this positivity journey. However, avoid toxic positivity at all costs, and that includes the people who engage in it. I've come across many toxic positive people on my travels, and they are extremely fake. They put on a front for the world, but deep down, they're terribly miserable, and that's not who you want to become.

Now that you're on your way to getting your mind right, it's time to take things to the next level and get your house in order. I'll tell you why in Chapter 4.

CHAPTER 4:

THE POWER OF ORDER: GET YOUR HOUSE ORGANIZED

"Getting organized is a sign of self-respect."
~Gabrielle Bernstein

When I started my healing journey, it seemed as if everything was going well. I was reading a lot of books, working on my mental health, and I was deep into writing my first book. But for some reason, I felt as if something was blocking me from reaching my full potential, and I couldn't figure it out. I had a chat with my mentor, James, and he agreed to come over to my apartment to investigate the issue further. This was the first time he had been to my place, and as soon as he walked in the door—I mean, he hadn't even sat down—he said, "You need to give this apartment a deep clean." I was pretty offended, as I thought my apartment was tidy enough. As far as I was concerned, everything was where it was supposed to be; it was a lot cleaner than the homes of most men I knew. But not according to James. He slowly walked around the flat, opening cupboards, closets, the fridge, and running his finger over the dust that had accumulated on the tops of cabinets. After he had completed his inspection, he sat me down and had a long discussion with me about the importance of cleanliness and order. He recommended a few books I should read, and he left. What James said made sense, but I wanted to look into it myself, and so I bought the books and read them—and boy was I shocked. What I learned and put into practice changed my life. And that's what I want to discuss in this chapter.

What Clutter Does to Your Mental Health

Let's start by defining clutter. Clutter is all the things in your home that do not have a home. The clothes that are hanging on the back of your door because there's no space in the closet. The saucepans sitting on the kitchen counters because there's no space in the cupboards. The books that are stacked on the end of the dining table because you don't have a bookshelf. It's the drawer full of junk that you keep filling up because it's easier to throw stuff in there. Clutter is the stuff you know you don't need but don't know what to do with. It's easy for things to pile up because we are constantly buying stuff we don't need. I was guilty of always giving in to the two-for-one bargains on things like cleaning products and tinned foods when I didn't need them. I would then store them in the pantry or cupboard and never use them. I was always buying clothes I didn't need because the items were on sale, but I would never wear them.

People who are surrounded by clutter are extremely disorganized, and it's often a sign of an underlying problem. Mine was stress and procrastination. I could never bring myself to start anything because I was just too stressed, and so I dealt with things by stashing everything away. Once I organized my home,

I simplified my life and things began to flow effortlessly, and I found that I was more energetic and happy. What I learned was that clutter has a negative effect on your mental health. Here's how:

Affects Your Mood: Clutter has a negative effect on your mood. Looking at all the things you know need your attention is frustrating. But that frustration is compounded when you just don't have the energy to do anything about it. This frustration leads to irritability, and when you feel irritated, you are tempted to do something to make you feel less irritated. For me, that was scrolling through social media or watching YouTube videos. But it was a vicious cycle, because after spending hours glued to the screen, I got even more frustrated because I couldn't manage to get anything done.

Increases Stress: Your stress levels increase when you are surrounded by clutter. You know you need to clean up the mess but there is so much of it that you get overwhelmed and don't touch it. The more you're exposed to clutter, the more stressed you get.

Steals Your Energy: Combined with healthy eating, I noticed a huge difference in my energy levels when I got my house in order. When I came home from work to a tidy house, it motivated me to do the things I needed to do to achieve my goals. When everything was in the right place, I was able to access the energy of abundance; it flowed through my home naturally and I was able to tap into it. On the other hand, when my house was full of clutter, I would come home, kick my shoes off, lie on the sofa, order a takeout and remain there until it was time to go to bed. Basically, clutter is a physical distraction that is mentally overwhelming and leads to increased anxiety and stress. These uncompleted tasks form a subconscious strain that depletes your energy without you realizing it.

Out of Control: Feeling that you are in control of your life is essential to your success. When there is too much stuff in your house and, as far as you are concerned, not enough hours in the day to organize everything, your stress levels soar and you feel as if you have no control over your life.

Feeling Defeated: When you believe a project is too big for you, you feel defeated. You look at it from so many different angles, wondering how you can complete it, but you can't see how you are going to do it. The problem is that the longer you leave it, the worse it gets, and eventually, you just give up altogether.

Affects Your Thinking: The negative feelings associated with clutter will begin to affect your mind. The thought of everything you need to get done to turn your house into a comfortable home can put a strain on your mind. It can even cause you to start having negative thoughts about yourself. Clutter has no place in your home, and nor does it have any place in your mind.

Decision Fatigue: When you're forced to make too many decisions, your decision-making skills diminish. This is known as decision fatigue and it can make life very difficult. The overwhelming effects of clutter cause decision fatigue. When you look at the mess, you don't even know where to start. A cluttered home equals a cluttered mind.

It's a Distraction: Clutter is a form of distraction. When I was trying to get stuff done, I would look up and see a pile of something that I needed to put away. But instead of putting it away, I would think about the fact that I needed to put it away and then try to get to what I was doing. However, the distraction made me lose focus, and before I knew it, I was talking on the phone or scrolling.

Causes Anxiety: The sight of a cluttered house makes you anxious; it causes nervousness and overwhelm, which shuts down the mind and body. The more anxious you feel, the less likely you are to get your house in order.

Encourages Unhealthy Eating: I found that I ate more junk food when my kitchen was a mess. I would use the excuse that all the pots and pans were dirty and so, to avoid starvation, I didn't have any choice but to order a takeout. Clutter is a downward spiral of decline. I couldn't be bothered to wash the dishes because I had no energy. Eating unhealthy food drained my energy even further, and I would end up eating takeout for weeks at a time because my kitchen was always a mess.

Low Self-Esteem: Having a cluttered house makes you feel bad about yourself. You know you need to tidy up, but you keep putting it off. The more you ignore the problem, the worse it gets. When friends come around, they mention it, and this makes you feel embarrassed. This feeling of embarrassment affects your self-esteem. The more your self-esteem is affected, the less confidence you have, and the less likely you are to clean up the clutter, and it becomes a vicious cycle.

Causes Depression: Recently, a friend of mine was struggling with depression. When I went over to his house, it was a mess! This was worse than clutter; it was absolutely disgusting! I didn't ask how he could have let his house get into such a state because I understood what was going on. If you don't get rid of clutter, all of its negative effects accumulate, and eventually you will end up depressed. So, it's best to get on top of it now before it takes complete control over your life.

Now you have a clear understanding about how clutter affects you negatively, let's take a look at how your life will improve when you organize your home.

- You will experience more joy and freedom in your life and home.

- You will experience a sense of calm and feel that you have more control over your life.

- Your stress levels will go down.

- You will have more energy to do the things that are important to you.

- Your ability to focus will improve.

- Your ability to process information will improve.

- You will have a clear mind, which will make it easier for you to make decisions.

- You will feel hopeful and empowered.

Get Decluttering Today

Living the life of your dreams and becoming the best version of yourself is a process, and a part of that process is getting your house in order. I can tell you from experience that decluttering your house is extremely difficult. As you walk into each room and realize how much work needs to be done, you'll get more and more overwhelmed. So, my advice to you is to start by creating a checklist. Write down everything that needs to get done, and as you complete each task, check it off your list. The key here is consistency. Whether it takes one month or six months, if you keep at it every day, even if it's just for half an hour, eventually you'll get it done. Here are some tips on how to get started:

Set Goals: One of the reasons people never achieve their goals is because they don't actually set them. As I mentioned, I made a New Year's resolution every year that I was going to write a book, and for several years I was unable to achieve that goal. Why? Because I didn't set the goal properly. It was wishful thinking, just an idea in my mind. Before you start tackling this mammoth task, work out exactly how you intend to do it. Here are some of the things you will need to take into consideration:

- Write down all the rooms you want to declutter and the areas in those rooms that need the most decluttering.

- Grade each area on the severity of the clutter. For example, if your bedroom is seriously junky, give it a five; if not, give it a two. The aim here is start in the areas with the most mess. By tackling the worst areas first, you will be more motivated to finish.

- Tackle one area at a time. Start in one area or room and work on it until it's decluttered. Multitasking will confuse you and slow you down.

- Choose realistic deadlines for each area/room. By giving yourself a deadline, you are more likely to get the work done.

- Plan the times when it's most convenient for you. I suggest working on an area every day, even if it's just for five minutes at a time. Trust me, if you say you're going to work on it on the weekends, you'll never get it done.

Create a System: Establishing a sorting system before getting started will make the task a lot easier. It will prevent you from having a pile of items in the corner of the room once you've finished cleaning that you don't know what to do with. The method I found most helpful was the three-box method. Get yourself three large boxes and label them, "Put in storage," "Get rid of," and "Keep."

- **Put in Storage:** Only store seasonal items that you actually use sporadically. For example, winter boots, hats, and scarfs. You will wear these during the winter months, so keep them somewhere safe until you need them again.

- **Get Rid Of:** The "Get rid of" box is for items you're either going to donate, sell, or give away. After clearing the area, take these items to their destinations.

- **Keep:** The items you keep are the things you use in your daily life. Once you've cleared the space, give every item in this box a home.

Disposal Options: There are so many things you can do with items you don't want/need. Here are some additional options for the "Get rid of" box:

- **Freecycle/Donate:** You will have plenty of items in good condition that you can give to friends, family members, or charity stores. These items might include shoes, clothes, cooking utensils or other household items.

- **Recycle:** Recyclable paper, plastics, and glass can go into the recycling bin if you have curbside pickup in your area. If not, put everything into bags and take them to your nearest recycling spot.

- **Rent a Dumpster:** Some of your items will be too worn-out or damaged to donate, give away, or sell, so throwing them in the trash will be your only option. If you have a lot of stuff to get rid of, rent a dumpster. The company will deliver it to your driveway and pick it up when you're done.

- **Have a Garage Sale:** As the saying goes, "One man's trash is another man's treasure." Why not make some money out of the things you don't need by having a garage sale? Make some flyers, go around town and put them in everyone's mailboxes. You can make some decent money from a garage sale.

The 20/20 Method for Decluttering: Developed by The Minimalists, Ryan Nicodemus and Joshua Fields Millburn, the 20/20 method advises that you should get rid of an item if you can replace it in under 20 minutes and it won't cost more than $20 to replace it. Please bear in mind that this method won't solve every dilemma you have, especially with larger items, but it works wonders for the smaller items such as:

- **Toys:** Do your kids have an excessive number of toys that they no longer play with?

- **Small appliances:** Do you have old appliances in the back of your cabinets that you don't use anymore?

- **Clothes:** Say goodbye to ill-fitting or outdated clothes.

- **Kitchen items:** Do you have duplicate items like extra tin openers and potato peelers? One of each is enough.

- **Makeup:** What makeup items are taking up space on your dresser?

- **Books:** Unless you plan on reading certain books again, get rid of them.

- **Coffee mugs:** Everyone in your house should have one coffee mug, and keep four for guests.

The 12/12/12 Challenge for Decluttering: Decluttering my home was not something I was looking forward to in the slightest. But then I found out about the 12/12/12 decluttering challenge and I was inspired to give it a try. It was created by Joshua Becker, author of *The Minimalist Home: A Room-by-Room Guide to a Decluttered, Refocused Life.* The rules are simple and involve setting a timer for one-hour intervals, choosing twelve items to throw away, twelve items to donate, and twelve items to put in their rightful places. Keep doing this until every item in a room has been organized. I found this to be a great challenge because it encouraged quick decision-making (the timer creates a sense of urgency), and it made me a lot more mindful of my possessions.

ADDITIONAL TIPS FOR DECLUTTERING YOUR HOME

Decluttering your home is a long and tedious process. Here are some additional tips to help make things easier:

- **Educate Yourself:** Read a book on decluttering such as *The Life-Changing Magic of Tidying Up* by Marie Kondo. I've read many books on decluttering, and I can tell you without a shadow of a doubt that this one is definitely life-changing—the title doesn't lie. Kondo instructs readers to throw out any items that don't give you a feeling of joy. During my research, I also learned that you should get rid of anything you haven't used for one year. The thought process behind this is that if you haven't used an item in one year, you are probably never going to use it.

- **Start with the Trash:** I started my decluttering process by taking the trash out. I went into each room with a black bag and picked up anything that looked like trash. This is a good place to start because it prepares you for the real decluttering since you don't have an emotional attachment to trash. It will also help you build momentum; once you get started, you'll be on a roll. As you move through your home throwing away trash, the volume of clutter you have to clear up will decrease.

- **Things You Think You Need:** If you scan your home, you'll find a lot of items you're keeping because you think you might need them sometime in the future. Get rid of these items, because you probably don't need them. Again, if you haven't used the item in a year, you're most likely not going to use it.

- **Photos and Paper:** In this digital era, there is no need to have stacks of photo albums and loads of paper such as receipts, bills, or coupons. Scan them all and throw the physical copies away.

- **Damaged Goods:** What damaged items are you holding on to because they've got sentimental value? That chipped mug your partner bought you? The broken necklace your grandmother gave you, or the worn-down shoes your best friend bought you for Christmas? These items are damaged and have no value; you couldn't even sell them for pennies, so you might as well get rid of them.

- **Duplicates/Extras:** Are you the type of person who buys things twice because they are on sale? You don't need the items, but because they were a cheap buy, you bought them again. If so, they're taking up unnecessary space—so get rid of them.

- **An Old Hobby:** Were you obsessed with tennis five years ago and bought loads of rackets, balls, and tennis equipment, but after an injury, you stopped playing, and now all your tennis equipment is collecting dust in the attic? If the stuff is in good condition, sell it; if not, bin it.

- **Anything Expired:** Go through your medicine cabinet, the fridge, pantry, and your make-up bag if you have one, and throw away anything that has expired. Firstly, it's bad for your health to use expired things, and secondly, they are taking up space.

- **Items from the Past:** Did you have a dog that died and you've kept things like their leash, water bowl, and toys? I know these items mean a lot to you, but if it's not too hard for you, please remove them from your home. You may also have clothes from a former profession such as a nurse, fireman, or veterinarian's uniform.

You can give these items to charity; people will even buy them as fancy-dress outfits.

- **Digital Clutter:** Your digital spaces may also need de-cluttering. Delete your emails, or put them in the necessary files. Your aim should be to get down to an empty inbox and keep it this way. Delete any music you no longer listen to, and unsubscribe from podcasts, newsletters, or anything else that no longer aligns with your current mental state.

Tips for Organizing Your Home

Your home will feel a lot lighter once it's decluttered. You will then need to organize it. How you choose to organize your home is up to you, but here are some tips that I found extremely helpful:

Door Racks: Storage racks on the backs of your bedroom, bathroom, and laundry-room doors help create a lot of extra space.

Trays on Dresser Tops: My dresser tops were always a mess; there was stuff flung everywhere, and I could never find anything. Trays simplify your life—they are durable, washable, and allow you to store items like jewelry, sunglasses, hairbands, combs/brushes, and other bits and bobs you would usually leave on your dressing table.

Mini Wastebasket: I used to trip over junk mail anytime I walked through my entryway because there was so much of it lying around. Putting a mini wastebasket in my hallway gave me somewhere to toss my mail as soon as I entered the front door.

Pillows/Throws: As comfortable as pillows and throws are, too many of them can make a room look junky, plus your guests won't have anywhere to sit. Instead, have a selection of no more than one throw and four pillows.

Toy Storage: If you've got kids, you can prevent your home from looking like a nursery by using regular storage bins for their toys. They are easy to clean, durable, and keep your space looking like adults actually live there.

Cleaning Products: Store your cleaning products in see-through multi-purpose bins. Buy the ones that are deep enough for tall bottles. You can then place the bins under the kitchen sink.

Decorative Box: A nice decorative box to hold things like hand cream, lip balm, sleeping masks, and earplugs will keep your bed area organized. Put one on your nightstand or on the floor by your bed.

Divided Turntables: Divided turntables are fantastic for awkward spaces. They are great for storing cleaning supplies or condiment bottles. The swivel effect gives you easy access to your items.

Labels: Don't neglect using labels; they will save you a lot of time when you need to find something in a hurry. Labeling is also very helpful when you live with other people.

Deep Drawers: If you're going to buy any new furniture, be sure to install large drawers. They make it easier to space out your items so that nothing gets lost in the back.

Tiered Spice Rack: With a tiered spice rack, you'll never need to empty your kitchen cabinets again in search of that one jar of curry powder. As long as you label them, a tiered spice rack makes all your spices visible.

Knife Organizer: A knife organizer is a safe way to store your knives and keep them off the counters. They lie in the drawers, giving you easy access to your knife collection when you need it.

Mount Hooks: In most homes, coat closets take up too much space, and our outer garments often end up thrown over chairs or on the ends of our beds. Hooks near your bedroom and front door make the coat-hanging process a lot more convenient, and it's a lot easier to grab your coat when you're leaving the house.

Clear Storage: Put miscellaneous items in clear storage containers. These are the small things that can't be grouped but tend to pile up on different tables around the house.

Pegboard: A pegboard wall helps you organize things like home-improvement tools, gym equipment, and cooking utensils.

Shelves: Build shelving units into the wall so you can organize your belongings more effectively and create more space.

Radiators: Don't be afraid to use the radiators for storage space during the summer months when they are turned off. Radiators are a great option for arranging potted plants, vases, and candles.

Windowsills: There are many household items you can place on windowsills to improve the organization of your home, such as collectibles, toy displays, books, and plants.

Gallery Wall: Do you have any photo frames lying around that you can make good use of? Put artwork or some nostalgic photos in them, and hang them up in a nice design on your wall.

Sideboards: Because we have so many large utensils, kitchens never seem to have enough space. Rollaway sideboards are a great way to store plates, bowls, and the kitchen appliances that take up the most space.

Stacking Bins: Make the most of vertical space under sinks by using stacking bins. You can store your first-aid, skin, body, and hair products in them.

Magazine Racks: Stylish magazine racks not only give your home a decorative touch, they're a great place to store smaller books and magazines in different rooms in the house.

Cord Organizers: Are you tired of tripping over cords? A cable-management box keeps excess cord lengths and power strips out of the way. You can also store your laptop and other cables in a tech pouch to keep them organized.

How to Maintain a Clutter-Free Home

When I grew up, my house was always immaculate because my mom didn't work outside the home. But things have drastically changed since then, and if you are married with children, you are most likely both working outside the home and have many obligations throughout the week, which makes it difficult to keep the house in order. Even with my obligations as a single man, I found it difficult to keep my apartment in order. But one of the main reasons for this was that I didn't have a system in place. So, before your house turns into a jungle again, here are some tips on how to maintain a clutter-free home:

Identify Bad Habits: Clutter doesn't accumulate because items have legs and find their way into piles all over your house. You are responsible for creating the clutter. What bad habits do you have that turn your home into a dumpster? Do you leave dishes in the sink all week? Do you leave dirty laundry all over the floor? How about letting boxes pile up from your online shopping? Whatever bad habits you have that lead to clutter building up, start working on replacing them with daily habits that will prevent your house from looking like a bomb has hit it every other week. Here are some good habits that will keep your living environment clutter-free:

- Do laundry once a week.
- Wash the dishes every night and as soon as you have used something in the kitchen.
- Sort out the mail every day.
- Put items back where you took them from.
- Don't move on to another project until you've completed the one you're working on.
- Put clean clothes in the closet and not on the back of a chair or on the floor.

Kids and Pets: Whether you have children already, you're expecting a baby, you have a pet, or you're about to buy one, make room for their stuff. Children and animals have toys, gadgets, and all types of play things that take up space in the house. Give all these items a home to prevent unnecessary clutter.

Store and Discard: You've just spent a few weeks getting your house in order by throwing out a lot of stuff. Don't let it all pile up again by buying things you don't need or not storing the things you do need in their rightful place. Keep an eye out for items that are taking up space for no reason and get rid of them.

Wise Storing: Store the things you use often where they are easy to reach so you're not making a mess of everything when you need them. Additionally, store the things you don't use often out of sight so you have more space available in your home. For example:

- Store your fine china on the top shelf.
- Use the attic or garage to store holiday decorations.
- Store sporting equipment in the garage.
- Store suitcases in the garage.
- Store everyday items where you can access them easily.

I remember the first time I walked through the door of my apartment after I had completely decluttered it. It felt so peaceful and it gave me the motivation I needed to really get to work on my goals. Everything was all good for a few weeks; I was washing the dishes after I had eaten, doing laundry once a week, and throwing away junk mail every day. But unfortunately, I fell back into my old habits and it didn't take long before my apartment looked like trash again. If being tidy is not one of your habits, expect to have a rollercoaster ride with keeping your house in order. The key is not to give up—because, like me, you'll get there in the end. Here's some inspiration for you: When I got consistent with keeping my apartment tidy, my book sales shot up. One of the things on my list of goals was to buy a house. I truly believe that unless you treat the things you already own with care, the universe won't make the shift required to get you the new things you want.

Now that your house is in order, it's time to really start working on your goals. But most people don't know how to set goals because they haven't been taught. Oscar-winning actor Denzel Washington once said, "Dreams without goals are just dreams and they ultimately fuel disappointment." There is a strategy to goal-setting, and without it, you won't succeed. Luckily, this strategy is no secret, and you can read all about it in Chapter 5.

CHAPTER 5:

WRITE THE VISION AND MAKE IT PLAIN: GOAL-SETTING WITH A PURPOSE

"A dream becomes a goal when action is taken towards its achievement."
—Bo Bennett

Have you ever attempted to drive to an unfamiliar destination without using a map or navigation system? I'm assuming that everyone will answer no to this question because it would be a complete waste of time and money and no one in their right mind would do such a thing. But just for a moment, I want you to imagine leaving your house knowing the address you want to go to but not knowing how to get there. You would end up driving around aimlessly, hoping and wishing to find the place. Unless you arrived there by fluke, after a few hours burning gas, you'd go back home. But what happens when you type the address into the navigation system? It gives you directions, so you leave your house, follow the directions, and arrive at your destination with no problems! The same rule applies to goal-setting.

As mentioned, 92% of people who set goals don't achieve them. That's because out of the 3% of Americans who do set goals, only 1% write them down and create a plan detailing how to achieve those goals. The people who don't create a plan are like the person in the car trying to get to a destination without directions—they drive around in circles and end up giving up. I used to be that person; as I've mentioned several times, every year, I would set a New Year's resolution to write my book. But I never wrote it down, and nor did I create a plan. However, as soon as I wrote my goal down and developed a plan for it, I wrote the book in less than a year. If you're tired of giving up on your goals because you don't know how to turn your dreams into a reality, I'm going to teach you how to set goals the S.M.A.R.T way.

Lifetime Goals: Most people live for the moment and they are not thinking about the future. But if you are serious about creating the life of your dreams, setting lifetime goals is essential. Have you not noticed how quickly time flies? I remember being in my 20s like it was yesterday, and because I didn't have a plan, my 30s slipped through my fingers. Before I knew it, I was almost 40 and dissatisfied with life.

I have a good friend called Charles. He is 25 years old and a multimillionaire commercial real estate developer. When I met him, I was slightly intimidated because when I was his age, I didn't have two pennies to rub together. I wanted to know how he became so wealthy. One day, over dinner, Charles told me his story. He comes from a very wealthy family; his father rents yachts to the rich and famous. His parents instilled discipline in him from a young age. As soon as he could read, he had to read one book a week and explain what the book was about to his parents. Reading became a habit, and to this day, he reads one book a week. From the age of five, Charles had to set three goals, create a vision board and a plan of how he intended on achieving those goals. Every year without fail, he achieved all three goals. He did chores for pocket money, and his dad encouraged him to save instead of spend, and make more money with the money that he had. At 13, he started a candy-selling business in school. He bought the candy at wholesale prices and set up a table outside his school selling candy cheaper than any of the stores in the area. He made no less than $300 a week.

Charles started several other profitable businesses during high school, and by the time he had finished, he had saved over $100,000. Instead of going to college, he got his real estate license—and the rest is history! Don't we all wish we had parents like Charles's? They taught him what they knew, he applied it, and he is living the life he envisioned for himself at 10 years old. Every action that Charles took, from the moment he wrote down his lifetime goals, prepared him to achieve them. Although he was so young, he knew exactly what he wanted, and he focused on it every year. While his peers were out having fun, Charles was working on his goals.

Goals are like an anchor; they prevent you from drifting. I spent the majority of my life drifting, and I only stopped when I started setting goals. Additionally, your goals are connected to your identity, and you will set them according to who you believe you are. It's also important to mention that goal-setting isn't just about achieving career or financial success; you can set goals for every area of your life. Here are some tips:

- **Education:** Do you want to go to college? Earn a master's or a doctorate degree? If you're already a graduate, what are your plans for continuous learning?

- **Family:** Do you want to get married and have children? If you already have a family, how do you intend on becoming a better parent and ensuring that you give your kids a better life than you had?

- **Financial:** How wealthy do you want to become? Do you want to save a certain amount of money each year?

- **Career/Business:** Do you want to climb the corporate ladder? If so, how high do you want to go? Do you want to start your own business? If so, what type of business do you want to start, and what level do you want to take it to?

- **Physical:** Do you want to transform your body through weight loss, or building muscle?

- **Attitude:** Is there anything about your character that you want to change? For example, are you too impatient? Do you have anger issues?

- **Public Service:** How do you feel you can contribute to the world? Do you want to become a volunteer? Maybe you have a passion for animals—you could volunteer in an animal shelter.

- **Pleasure:** All work with no play makes life very boring. How do you intend on enjoying life? Travel, spending time with friends and family, hobbies?

Set your lifetime goals for the next five to ten years. Get a pen and a notepad, find a quiet location where you won't be disturbed, and start brainstorming. It is not necessary to set goals for each section, but for the ones you do choose, set two to three goals for each. It's important to look deep within and work from the heart. Don't allow your family, friends, or society to influence your decisions. For example, let's say your parents expect you to take over the family business after you graduate college but you have no desire to do so. Don't make that one of your goals; in fact, plan when you intend on telling them that you won't be running the business because you have your own life goals you want to achieve. This is your life, you are the only one who has to live it, and it's about doing what makes you happy and no one else. It's important to mention that setting goals is not a onetime event. Once you achieve your goals, don't sit back and put your feet up—keep setting goals. The most successful people in the world, including sportspeople, entrepreneurs, and those in the entertainment industry, keep setting goals, despite having millions in the bank. Make a habit of setting goals, and watch your life flourish.

Break the Goals Down: In order to achieve your lifetime goals, you will need to break them down into smaller goals. Create a one-month, a six-month, and a one-year plan for each goal. Finally, create a daily to-do list of the things you will need to do each day to achieve these goals. For example, to start, you may need to gather information by doing things like reading books and watching videos to learn how to achieve your goals. Once you have everything written down, read over your plan to determine whether you need to make any changes.

Stay on Course: Keep reviewing and updating your to-do list to ensure you stay on course. Review your long-term goals and modify them if they no longer reflect your experiences and priorities. For example, after studying what is required to maintain a healthy marriage and raise children, you may decide that you would rather stay single.

S.M.A.R.T Goals: An effective way to achieve your goals is to apply the S.M.A.R.T goals method. There are several variants to this acronym, and one of them is:

- **S** – Specific
- **M** – Measurable
- **A** – Attainable
- **R** – Relevant
- **T** – Time-Bound

Even people who write their goals down often fail to achieve them because they are not specific. I will use myself as an example. One year, I wrote on a sticky note, "I will write a book" and stuck it on my computer screen. I read that goal every day for one year, but I still didn't manage to finish writing the book that year. Why? Because it wasn't specific. However, when I wrote, "I will write a book about the importance of believing in yourself by December 31st, 2004," I achieved my goal. Obviously, there was a lot more that went into successfully writing the book than just writing the goal down. But seeing a date every day gave my subconscious mind something to work towards—whereas when there was no date, my subconscious mind led me to believe I had all the time in the world to write the book.

Additional Goal-Setting Tips

Goal-setting is only effective when it is done the right way. Here are some additional tips to help you get the most out of goal-setting:

- **A Positive Statement:** Write out each goal as a positive statement. For example, write, "I am a healthy eater," not, "Stop being so undisciplined and eat less junk food."

- **Be Precise:** Add dates, timeframes, and amounts to your goals so you can measure your progress. For example, write, "I am going to save $500 per month," not, "I am going to save more money each month." If you manage to save $500 before the end of the month, you change the goal to, "I will save a minimum of $500 per month."

- **Set Priorities:** Most likely, you are going to have more than one goal. Don't overwhelm yourself by trying to achieve them all at the same time. Decide which goal is the most important, prioritize them, and work on one goal at a time.

- **Keep Them Small:** Make sure you break your goals down into the smallest components because it will make the overall goal easier to achieve. When I first started writing my book, I wrote 500 words a day until the book was complete. For me, it was easy to write 500 words, which is why I was able to sit down and write them every day; my subconscious mind didn't resist it. However, if I had attempted to write 2000 words per day, I doubt I would have had such a positive outcome.

- **Set Performance Goals:** Don't focus on the results; instead, set performance goals, because there will be times when you have no control over the results—however, you *do* have control over your performance. For example, instead of setting a goal to become the best tennis player in your district, set a goal to give everything you've got during training. In this way, you avoid disappointment because several factors could contribute to you not becoming the best tennis player in your district. For example, the person you are up against might just be stronger and more powerful than you. Or, on the day of the match, the bad weather may prevent you from performing at your best.

- **Set Realistic Goals:** I believe we are all capable of achieving any goal we set our minds to. However, setting unrealistic goals sets you up for failure. Let's say you are 200 lbs overweight, and you've just watched a silly video claiming that some new dynamic weight-loss pills will guarantee that you lose 100 lbs a month. Don't get tempted by the pills and set a goal to lose 100 lbs per month because, firstly, losing that much weight in such a short space of time is dangerous, and secondly, there's a high chance that it won't work and you're just setting yourself up for failure. Instead, set a realistic goal of losing 2 lbs a week or 8 lbs a month. In this way, not only are you more likely to achieve your weight-loss goals, you are also more likely to keep the weight off.

I felt so good when I had written down my goals and formulated a strategy for how I was going to achieve them. But the minute I got to work, I was bombarded with distractions and they held me back until I learned how to manage them. You are no different, my friend; every successful person speaks about their battle with distractions. I believe it's the universe's way of testing how badly you want what you say you want. The good news is that you can beat distractions. In Chapter 6, I'm going to teach you how to get rid of distractions and amplify your focus.

CHAPTER 6:

DITCH THE DISTRACTIONS: HOW TO MAINTAIN YOUR FOCUS

> *"Work is hard. Distractions are plentiful.
> And time is short."*
> ~Adam Hochschild

Now you've decided to change your life and start working to achieve your goals, the distractions will intensify and you will feel as if you're being attacked on every side. I can't tell you whether this is a universal principle or not, but I can tell you with confidence that you are going to be distracted. You will feel as if there are invisible hands pulling you away from achieving your goals. This is all a part of the process, and it is essential that you learn how to eliminate distractions and maintain your focus, or you won't be able to get anything done. I believe the only person capable of holding you back from success is *you*, and one of the quickest routes to failure is distractions and your inability to focus. You can't stop the distractions from coming, but you can learn how to prevent them from distracting you.

What Are Distractions?

I thought I'd start with defining the term *distractions* because I've learned along this journey that a lot of people don't actually know what they are. Distractions are the obstacles you encounter throughout your day that steer you in a different direction. It's your responsibility to take control of those distractions and refuse to allow your time to be stolen from you. It's about being completely focused on the road in front of you and not allowing anything to get in your way.

Today, being distracted is the norm. People laugh and joke about it all the time, but in reality, it's not funny. Whether it's social media, TV, friends, or family members, there is always something pulling us away from what really matters—our productivity, our focus, and our ability to get stuff done. It is extremely difficult to keep your eyes on the prize when you're surrounded by distractions. Imagine you're a boxer, and the day of your world championship fight there is not one opponent in the ring but ten, all throwing punches at you from different directions. There's no way you're going to win that fight. But that's what fighting against distractions is like. Instead of dodging the blows, we try and do everything at once. We have a fancy name for this; it's called *multitasking*. Everyone thinks it's cool to multitask because on the surface, it looks like we're getting loads of stuff done at once. However, the American Psychological Association states that when we bounce from task to task, we are 40% less productive because each time we move to a different task, the brain needs to redirect and readjust.

Additionally, distractions take up an average of 2.1 hours of our time every day. Sure, we know what the typical distractions are—phone notifications, kids wanting our attention, spouse wanting our attention, social media, and TV—but let's take a deeper look. When we are stressed, anxious, and worried, it affects our ability to concentrate. In this chapter, you will learn a lot more about these attention thieves and how to protect yourself against them.

Distractions are like that annoying fly buzzing around your head when you're trying to enjoy your dinner. You keep swatting it away, but it keeps coming back, and the only way to get rid of it is to kill it. To be more specific, according to the *Merriam Webster Dictionary*, a distraction is "Something that directs our attention away from something else." Distractions steal our focus, they snatch our attention, and then we are left saying things like, "There are not enough hours in the day." There are more than enough hours in the day. The problem is that we don't use them wisely. Distractions come in many forms. Here are some of the main culprits:

- **Notifications:** Our phones are probably our main source of distraction. They are constantly buzzing, pinging, and basically screaming at us to play with them. Each time you pick up your phone, your focus diminishes and your productivity plummets.

- **Email:** Checking your emails every hour is another sneaky distraction that knocks us off course. Emails don't seem like that big of a deal, but when there are messages you need to reply to, they can cause a major disruption.

- **Social Media:** Does this sound familiar: "Let me just check this one post"? And before you know it, you're mindlessly scrolling through your feed, hours have passed, and you haven't done anything you said you were going to do.

What Distractions Can Cost You

Distractions destroy productivity. On average, a person runs into a distraction every 11 minutes. It then takes them approximately 25 minutes to regain their focus. That means that out of every eight hours, you are wasting six of them to distractions. Here are some more disturbing statistics:

- Distractions cause 54% of people to underperform.

- Distractions make 50% of people a lot less productive.

- Distractions cause 20% of people not to climb the career ladder or reach their full potential.

- 45% of companies reported that distractions compromise the quality of their employees' work.

- 30% of companies reported that there is low morale in the office because the employees who are not distracted have to take on extra work to cover for the employees who are distracted.

- 25% of companies reported that distractions have a negative effect on employee/manager relationships.

- 24% of companies reported missed deadlines because of distractions.

- 21% of companies reported a revenue loss because of distractions.

Why Are People so Easily Distracted?

When discussing how to become successful, I always revert back to the fact that only 1% of people own 50% of the world's wealth. While there are most certainly other factors at play, I wholeheartedly believe that being easily distracted is one of the reasons people don't succeed. It takes a level of focus that most people know nothing about to achieve your goals. We'll get into this more later, but you've got to shut out the noise and have complete control over your mind to have laser-sharp focus. Because, trust and do believe, your mind will turn on you and tell you to do things that feel good so you can escape your task. You've got to have the mental capacity to be able to say no. Let's take a look at why we are so easily distracted.

Hardwired Brains: Neurological research has found that humans don't have continuous streams of concentration available to them, and that our brains are hardwired to respond to distractions. People work best in a series of short bursts, but when they take a break, they get distracted. The brain scans the surroundings looking for something more stimulating to do. If you can't find anything, you'll go back to what you were doing. But not before losing precious time being distracted.

That's the Way of the World: I personally don't believe there will ever be another Albert Einstein or Isaac Newton because the world is too full of distractions that actually slow the brain down. Research suggests that too much scrolling can be neurologically damaging. It has the same impact on our brains as age-related cognitive decline! That's pretty serious—the more you scroll, the faster your brain ages. The problem is we live in a world where excessive scrolling is the norm. We even see toddlers swiping as their mothers wheel them around supermarkets frantically shopping while they too are scrolling!

While the advance in technology has done wonders for the world, it has also caused and is causing a lot of damage. Technology has become a double-edged sword. I remember the days when we had to handwrite our college papers. Now we can type them and cut by half the time it takes to write them. But while technology boosts our productivity, it has also proven to be a major distraction. Here are a few statistics that highlight how bad the situation really is:

- 84.4% of people say they are distracted at work.
- 26% said the distraction comes from emails.
- 55% said the distraction comes from texts and phone calls.
- 27% said the distraction comes from the Internet.
- 41% said they are distracted by entertainment.

A study conducted by the University of Florida provides us with some more insight into our battle with distractions. Researchers found that, depending on what we are exposed to, our brain waves vibrate at different frequencies. When exposed to automatic stimuli, the rhythm speeds up, but when we make a conscious decision to focus on a task, the brain slows down. In a world filled with distractions, this makes it even more difficult to maintain focus. Imagine this scenario: you're deeply engaged in a project, and your phone pings with a notification. On the surface, that beep is insignificant because it's a tiny little noise. But it is loud enough to disrupt your ability to concentrate. Once you've checked your phone, even if it was nothing, getting back to the same level of focus is now virtually impossible.

But when we discuss the issue of distractions with our friends, we all laugh and joke about it. Our phones have become a socially acceptable form of addiction, and there are very few people who are willing to do the work to overcome it because it's just too hard.

Short Attention Spans: Our brains are intricate and brilliant machines; however, they have a very odd quirk of drifting away when we should be focused on something important. A Harvard University study found that our minds are in a different location 47% of the time. In other words, most of us believe we are focused on a task, but the reality is that our thoughts are roaming around in another realm. This is not because we are not committed or lack interest in the task at hand—it's because our attention span has a limit. Similar to a fuel tank; when the fuel is empty, the car stops running. With humans, once we've got no more attention to give, we start looking for something else to do, and that's typically something that's easier on the brain.

Think about what happens when you have a task to complete that's going to take hours of your time, and you need to give it your complete attention. You will start off enthusiastic about the project with the ability to concentrate on it deeply. But as the clock starts ticking, your mind will start wandering. It's not a sign that you are not committed to the project—it's just how humans respond to monotony. We might get bored, need a break, or require stimulation from something else. Basically, it's normal to have a short attention span; it's not a flaw. However, to create effective strategies to work with it instead of against it, you must first recognize that you have a short attention span.

Poor Time Management: Time management is not something they teach us in school. The average person is not taught how to manage their time efficiently; it's a skill that most people, including myself, had to learn by ourselves. And I don't know about you, but it took me a long time to master it. I wasted a lot of time and missed a lot of opportunities because I had bad time-management skills. This is a recipe for disaster because it opens the door to distractions and hinders productivity. Without priorities or a clear goal to work on, you will struggle to stay focused and easily get sidetracked by things that are not important. Not being able to divide your time wisely will have you bouncing between tasks and getting consumed by minor details. Additionally, effective time management fuels productivity, because if you don't know where to start, you'll sit around twiddling your thumbs for hours on end.

How to Be Less Distracted and Maintain Your Focus

As you've read, distractions are everywhere; we can't prevent them. But we *can* prevent them from distracting us. Very few distractions need our immediate attention, and the majority of them are nowhere near as important as they appear to be. Distractions are not just irritating interruptions that disrupt what we're doing—they are a choice. Most people allow distractions into their lives because they simply don't have the self-discipline required to keep them out. But you have more control over your ability to focus than you think. Here are some tips on how to be less distracted and maintain your focus.

Eliminate External Distractions: What are your main distractions? Is it the TV, your phone, or your kids? Turn off your TV and phone; if your children are a distraction, wake up earlier so you can work while they're asleep. What does the wall in front of your desk look like? Is it full of pictures and trinkets? Take them down because they can cause your mind to stray. Just looking up at the wall every few minutes can take you down memory lane, and before you know it, you've spent an hour daydreaming. Take a few minutes to take inventory of your physical environment and get rid of anything that could distract you.

Have a Plan: Whether you do this the night before or first thing in the morning, create a plan for how your day should go. Whether you use a time-management app or you write everything down in a notebook, list your tasks in order of importance. Are there any tasks you can delegate or cross off your list altogether? The elimination category could include things like responding to emails, or answering questions from your team. Make sure you follow through with everything on your list and don't allow anyone or anything to stand in your way. When you start your day with a clear head, knowing exactly what to do, you are more likely not to give in to distractions.

Be Selective: If you're a workaholic like me, you will want to get as many tasks done as possible by the end of your working day. When I first started on my journey, I would put 20 items on my to-do list and kill myself trying to get them done. But guess what—I never got them all done. Why? Because when you put yourself under too much pressure, your focus decreases and your productivity levels are not that great. When your mind is focused on 20 different projects, you can't concentrate on any of them.

To win your battle with distractions, it is important to have as few items on your to-do list as possible. I've found 2–3 works for me—any more and I burn myself out. At first, it will seem counterproductive—why only work on 2–3 projects when you've got so much to do? But there are several benefits associated with narrowing your focus. Don't confuse being productive with getting everything done as soon as possible. Instead, take slow, deliberate steps towards getting stuff done. Consistency is better than intensity. By being too intense, you will burn yourself out. However, with a slow and steady pace, you will stay in the game and win.

Additionally, when you have too many tasks on your list and you don't finish them, you feel defeated, and you will start losing confidence in yourself. Intensity is not good for your mental health. As you take the slow and steady approach, you'll start seeing progress, which will motivate you to keep going.

Block Time: To ensure you get your 2–3 tasks done, block out a time for them. As mentioned, distractions come in all forms, from a child demanding your attention, to an unexpected email, or a co-worker needing your help. Any of these interruptions can steal your willpower and make it difficult for you to focus on your tasks. However, by giving yourself a certain time to finish each task, you will refuse to allow anything to interrupt you because you know you've only got a few hours to complete the task. Research suggests that when people give themselves deadlines, or set timers, they are more likely to accomplish everything they need to get done within that allotted timeframe.

Split Tasks: Large tasks are depressing. They appear like a large mountain in front of you that is impossible to get over. What typically happens when you have a large goal is:

- You waste time daydreaming about how good it will feel when you've achieved the goal.

- The goal seems too big and you don't feel confident that you'll achieve it.

Thinking about a large goal is an enemy to your focus. When you keep looking at the bigger picture, you set yourself up for failure. Instead, break your large goal into small, manageable tasks that you can work on daily. For example, let's say you're a manager and you've got to interview 20 new employees for their probationary period and write out their reports. This is a lot of work, and the thought of it is daunting. However, if you've been given three months to get it done, you can break the task down so you're doing two interviews every other day, and every other day you're doing two write-ups. You'll have the entire project complete within the 60 days, and it will be nowhere near as stressful as it would have been if you had attempted to do it all at once.

Reel-It-In Method: As mentioned, distractions are not just external; they are also internal. It's not that you're not fully committed to the task, but you might be dealing with some inner conflict you're trying to run away from. When you hear birds chirping at the window, you look up and investigate, not because you want to escape from your work, but because you want to escape from yourself. However, when you urgently need to use the restroom, what happens? No amount of emails, text messages, or social media posts can stop you from going to the bathroom. You put everything on hold and go because your mind and body has a clear understanding of the task at hand. All of a sudden you have an instinctive laser-like focus. The decision to use the toilet is made subconsciously. Imagine being able to apply this same intense concentration to your daily tasks!

    The thing is that there are some distractions you can control, and there are some you can't. The key is to gain an advantage over these. The most effective strategy to achieve this is the "reel-it-in method." This method isn't simply about working around the distractions, but about using those distractions as a tool to sharpen your focus. You can use the reel-it-in method for any distractions, including the internal ones where your mind takes a trip to South Africa while you are in New York. It's about choice—you *choose* whether you are going to submit to the distraction or not. This method equips you to be consistent in making the right choices. Each distraction gives you the opportunity to strengthen your decision-making skills. Rather than the distractions having control over you, you will have control over the distractions. Each time you choose to ignore the distractions, your focus will improve. Sounds simple enough, right? Unfortunately, it isn't—but it is possible. You've just got to keep trying. Here are the three steps to implement the reel-it-in method:

Step 1: Mental Housekeeping: Start by visualizing what a normal day looks like when you're interrupted. It might be a social media post, an email, or a text message from a friend. Or, your inner world might distract you, such as a lingering thought, a sudden memory, or a worrying situation you're dealing with. Normally, you would give in to the distraction. But in this visualization, I want you to stop and become mindful of your situation by doing the following:

- Sit comfortably with your eyes closed to disconnect from what's taking place around you.

- Breathe in deeply through your nose; feel your lungs filling up with air and hold your breath for five seconds.

- Breathe out slowly while imagining that your mind is releasing all the negative things it's holding on to.

Repeat this exercise as many times as you need to until your mind is clear.

Step 2: Be Present: Now that your mind is clear, the next step is to get present by grounding yourself. Imagine that your mind has several lines protruding out of it. These lines are reaching towards your worries, reminders, and thoughts. While in a fight for your attention, these things cause you to lose focus. Now, imagine those lines are like a fisherman's rod and you are reeling them back in. The lines you reel in represent a piece of your attention coming back to you. You are collecting all your thoughts and regaining your focus. Quietly say to yourself, "This moment is the only thing that matters."

Stepping into the present moment is essential because the present is all we have. The past is gone, we can't reclaim it, and the future is yet to come. They are a figment of our imagination. The present is the only space in time we can affect. Here are some questions to help guide you back to the present moment:

- Is this something I will regret doing later?

- Are there any reasons why I need to care about this?

- Do I need to pay attention to this immediately? Is it urgent?

- Is there anything of extreme importance I could be doing right now?

- What can I do right now that will be a good use of my time?

- Why am I doing what I'm doing right now?

By asking yourself these questions, you will be capable of discerning the importance and the urgency of the distraction. They will allow you to make an intelligent decision as to whether to acknowledge the distraction or continue with what you are doing. The main goal is to ensure that every second of your time is used wisely and that you are productive in your endeavors.

Step 3: Make a Choice: You need to process a distraction before you can address it, which requires you to make a decision about it. Unless you address it, the distraction will return and bug you until you do something about it. By making a decision, you will have peace of mind. Here are some tips on how to make a decision about a distraction:

- **Write a To-Do List:** Let's say you get a phone notification. Instead of clicking on it, write down that you need to check it. Once you've got the task down on paper, your mind can relax because you've told it that you've noted the distraction and you will address it when you're ready.

- **Allocate Time:** Allocate time during the day to address the tasks on your to-do list. For example, you might give yourself 30 minutes after your tea break and another hour after dinner to address everything on the list. The goal is to prevent the list from becoming overwhelming by taking time to clear it throughout the day. Remember, it's not about ignoring the distraction, but about recognizing it and carving out time to address it later on in the day. You can then return to what you were doing.

By allocating time to tend to your distractions, you are turning them into tasks, while remaining productive and ensuring that everything receives the attention it needs.

You and only you are responsible for keeping distractions to a minimum. Friends and loved ones will feel like you're shutting them out when you don't respond to their messages immediately or they can't reach you because your phone is on "do not disturb," but don't allow them to guilt-trip you. If you want to be successful, these are the sacrifices you'll need to make. Speaking of sacrifices, let's discuss this more in Chapter 7.

CHAPTER 7:

GO ALL OUT: FORGET ABOUT WORK-LIFE BALANCE FOR NOW

"The key is not to prioritize what's on your schedule, but to schedule your priorities."
~Stephen Covey

"Oh, my goodness, you need a break." "It's not healthy to work as hard as you do." "Did you know that overworking causes heart conditions?" These were the comments my friends and family made when I started getting serious about achieving my goals. While I know they had my best interests at heart, they had no idea the level of self-sacrifice and hard work it takes to achieve your goals. Of course I tuned out the noise and kept it moving; however, it was annoying nonetheless. I really want you to understand how important it is to prioritize your goals and stop listening to friends and family. No shade, no tea, but they most likely haven't achieved anything in life, and probably never will. The bottom line is that you can't afford to listen to people who haven't reached the level of success you're aspiring to. Going on vacation and shopping sprees should be the last thing on your mind right now. This season of your life is going to be difficult, but I can assure you that once you achieve your goals, you'll look back and say it was all worth it. For now, I want you to forget about work-life balance.

What Does a Healthy Work-Life Balance Look Like?

The world is obsessed with having a healthy work-life balance; it's being discussed on the news, social media, and every media outlet there is. But why is it so important, and what does a healthy work-life balance look like?

Well, let me speak for myself first. When I had a 9–5 job, I was obsessed with having a healthy work-life balance because I hated my job and the extra effort I had to put in if I wanted to be seen as a "good employee" and get promoted for more pay—which technically wasn't more pay because you would be working more hours. My friends and I would spend a lot of time on the phone complaining about the extra hours we were asked to work and how we were not paid overtime. For us, the difference between working until 6:00 p.m. instead of 5:00 p.m. was astronomical. It meant that I was stuck in rush-hour traffic for two hours instead of one. By the time I got home, I was exhausted and unable to do anything except watch TV, scroll, and talk on the phone. Working in a job I hated was a nightmare. Even if I had been able to leave at 5:00 p.m. every day, I doubt I would ever have been able to say I had a healthy work-life balance because the reality of the situation was that whether I left work at 5:00 p.m. or 6:00 p.m., I did the same thing—waste my evening doing unproductive stuff. So, where was the balance?

I don't believe a healthy work-life balance exists when you don't like your job because there is nothing healthy about not liking your job—and according to research, 45% of American workers wouldn't wish their job on their worst enemy! Therefore, the problem isn't about balance, but about job satisfaction. So, to me, a healthy work-life balance means being satisfied with the work you do and satisfied with the life you are living. Without both, you will never have a healthy work-life balance. But let's take a look at what it means to other people.

Research suggests that 60% of employees in the United States don't believe they have a healthy work-life balance. The reason for this is that they are working too much and not playing enough. Nevertheless, the general consensus is that a healthy work-life balance means you should be giving equal amounts of energy to your work and your personal life. There should be no difference between the two. You shouldn't be so drained from your personal life that you can't perform at work, and nor should you be so drained from your professional life that you have no time for friends and family. A healthy work-life balance is about having the ability to fulfil both personal and professional commitments at the same time as prioritizing your physical and mental well-being.

The ideal work week would mean that after work, people have time to do the things they enjoy, such as engage with friends and family, or participate in a hobby. A healthy work-life balance could also include the following:

- **Time Management:** Being able to organize your time effectively between work responsibilities, family time, friends, hobbies, and personal pursuits without feeling burned out.

- **Setting Boundaries:** Setting boundaries involves ensuring that your work life does not spill over into your personal life. For example, you don't take work home, or tolerate your manager calling you out of hours.

- **Flexibility:** Being able to adjust and adapt your schedule to handle personal needs or unforeseen circumstances without it being a problem at work.

- **Stress Management:** Having time to practice stress-management tactics such as mindfulness, yoga, physical activities; being able to take breaks and unplug from the demanding nature of the work environment.

According to experts, a healthy work-life balance is important for our physical and mental well-being. If this is not prioritized, it can lead to burnout, a lack of self-care, and a neglected personal life. However, despite how long we've been having this conversation, more than half of the American workforce don't have a healthy work-life balance. Why is this? I believe that as long as people hate their jobs, they can never have a healthy work-life balance—which is why I need you to forget about it for now.

Why You Should Forget About Having a Healthy-Work Life Balance for Now

If you want to have the perfect work-life balance and become successful, you might as well shut this book right now and accept that you are going to work a 9–5 for the rest of your life. Let me start by talking about myself. Success requires a lot of sacrifice, and this was a lesson I learned very quickly when I started writing my first book. To stay consistent, I had to say no to going out on Friday and Saturday nights and partying. Those hangovers would always set me back a couple of days, and it would take me about two weeks to find my flow again. The first time I realized how disruptive going out was, I started saying no to all invitations. Of course, my friends and family were not happy about it. In fact, I eventually lost most of my friends (more on that later). I also had to temporarily ditch my hiking hobby. But I knew I wanted to quit my unfulfilling job and become an independent author. I knew there was no way this was going to happen if I was going out all the time. For one, it takes extreme focus to write a book, and second, it's expensive, there is so much that goes into publishing a book, and when you are covering those expenses yourself, you've got to save money. One of the ways I saved money was to stop going out.

No, I wasn't working myself into the ground and taking no breaks—I just had a very strict system. I wrote for 30 minutes in the morning and for three hours in the evening. On Saturdays, I wrote for 10 hours, and on Sundays, I took a break. Typically, that break was on the sofa reading a book. I disciplined myself to go out once a month to see family or friends, and I would always meet up with people in the early afternoon so I could come home and get ready for work on Monday. My system worked for me: I felt chilled, content, and happy knowing I was making a lot of progress.

Earlier, I spoke about what a balanced life looks like, and I mentioned that people are always striving for the perfect work-life balance. Well, I'm not a fan of the term *work-life balance* because it implies that your work and life are two separate entities. That's what society has convinced us to believe—that we work for the system, and then go home to be with our families. But as far as I'm concerned, work is life, and life is work. However, you will only get to this point once you've found your life's purpose. I only consider my work *work* because it pays me. However, to me, my work is my life. I love what I do, and it's connected to every part of my being.

People desire to have a fulfilling life outside of work because they are unhappy in their place of employment. These are the people who dread getting out of bed every morning, who hate their managers and their co-workers, and live for Fridays. I know because I used to be like that. I absolutely loathed my job. Self-employed people have a different mindset. For us, work is wonderful. We love creating, building, learning, and taking risks. While the self-employed journey is difficult, I would rather struggle building something that belongs to me than struggle working to turn someone else's dream into reality.

Most people would describe their ideal life as financially free, full of love, happiness, and success. Let me stress again, you will never achieve this working a 9–5 job unless you are investment-savvy and know how to make your money work for you. That's why starting your own business is the only way out of the rat race, and there is no balance on this side of the fence. Despite the fact that everyone wants to be successful, the road to success is often demonized. We are referred to as workaholics, people who are incapable of thinking about anything but work. This causes poor health, broken relationships, and stress. However, a work-is-life mindset is not the same. Despite how difficult it can be, we love what we do; our business is all we think about, and we are constantly getting inspired by new ideas and our surroundings.

In the beginning, when you are building the foundation of your business, you will need to drastically tone down your social life. But once things are up and running, you can really start enjoying life. I've traveled to over 20 countries, I volunteer, I go out with friends, and I spend time with family. People are always asking me how I can have so much fun at the same time as running such a successful publishing company. My answer has always been a simple one: my life is my work, and my work is my life. I will write chapters of a book on a plane, and take conference calls on the beach. You will never stop me from working.

So this is where it gets serious, guys—making the decision to ditch the idea of having a healthy work-life balance. To really take hold of what you want out of life, you will need to work a 9-5, come home, and work on your dreams. Don't ask me how long this will take because I can't tell you how long it will take for *your* dreams to manifest. But what I *can* tell you is that every successful person I know, including myself, spent several years working on their dreams before they truly reaped the benefits. Basically, if you're not prepared to put in some years of painstaking hard work and sacrifice, you're traveling on the wrong road.

Next, I want to talk to you about motivation because there are so many misconceptions about it that if you don't understand how it works, you will give up on your dreams before you've even reached first base.

CHAPTER 8:

MOTIVATION IS NOT ENOUGH: HOW TO KEEP GOING WHEN YOU DON'T FEEL IT

"Success is not final; failure is not fatal; it is the courage to continue that counts."
—Winston Churchill

Motivation is an emotion, and it's not going to be the driving force behind your success. Because motivation is an emotion, it's fleeting. Have you ever watched a motivational film, listened to a speech or a song, and felt all fired up and ready to start working on your goals? After watching *The Pursuit of Happiness*, I was so motivated that I immediately packed my bag and went to the gym in the middle of the night. But two days later, I was back to my old habits of eating takeout and pigging out on the sofa in front of the TV. What happened? I wasn't motivated anymore. So, what do you do when your motivation runs out? Keep working!

What Is Motivation?

Motivation is something that takes place inside of us. Some experts describe it as a drive; others describe it as a need. Either way, it is a mental state connected to change. When we are motivated, we are fueled with the energy required to do the work necessary to achieve our goals. Motivation fuels all sorts of behaviors, such as the need to eat, drink, get the body of your dreams, attract the opposite sex, and much more. Sounds simple enough, right? But it's not. There are two types of motivation: extrinsic and intrinsic.

- **Extrinsic Motivation:** Extrinsic motivation is about the reward we are going to receive for doing something. These rewards can include money, a promotion, or avoiding punishment. Extrinsic motivation motivates us to do what is required of us so we can get what we want.

Intrinsic Motivation: Intrinsic motivation involves completing a task because we want to. It gives us a sense of satisfaction, and we enjoy doing it. People who are intrinsically motivated are not thinking about external rewards.

Now, I want you to cast your mind back to the last time you had something to do and you failed to do it. Maybe you decided to start practicing meditation every morning, or to submit an application for a job before the deadline. Did you fail to do it because you had decided that it didn't matter anymore? That's not the case for most people. A lack of motivation was the reason you didn't do what you said you were going to do. As mentioned, motivation is an emotion, and it doesn't show up because you need it. So, as you've probably learned while lying on your sofa scrolling through social media, no magical sensation is going to arrive to get you up and working—it's *your* job to motivate yourself.

When I realized how unmotivated I was, I panicked. I believed I was never going to become successful because I wasn't on fire all the time. There were many times when I literally had to drag myself off the couch to get stuff done. But that's because it's in our nature to take the path of least resistance. In his book *The Path of Least Resistance,* Robert Fritz states that human beings are no different to the elements in nature. He states that energy moves along the path on which it is easiest to travel. The water in a river doesn't flow upstream; it flows downstream. The wind blowing through trees takes the path of least resistance, as do electrical currents, no matter what they are flowing through. However, the difference between us and nature is that we have a choice as to which direction to take. Success is hard, and most people who say they want to be successful quickly give up when they realize how much work goes into it. You are not skipping through a bed of roses to get what you want—you are going to have to claw your way to the top.

THINGS THAT AFFECT YOUR MOTIVATION

While it's true that motivation runs out and you are not always going to have a burning desire to attack your goals, there are things that will strip you of your motivation completely, and no matter how much you try to will yourself to get moving, you won't be able to. Here are a few things that might be affecting your motivation:

You Have No Plan: Having no plan is the biggest motivation killer. I had no idea how to write a book, and so I would sit behind my computer and just start writing. But because I didn't know which direction to take, and how to put everything together, I didn't get very far. I quickly realized how true Benjamin Franklin's quote was: "If you fail to plan, you are planning to fail." No matter what you want to achieve, you need to know what path to take to get you there. Here are some of the main benefits associated with planning:

- **Gives You Direction:** To remain on track and to stay motivated, you need direction—and planning helps you achieve this. Just setting a goal that you want to lose weight without creating a meal plan or an exercise plan will set you up for failure very quickly. When you know you want to lose 2 lbs per week and you know exactly how many calories to cut out and how much exercise to do, your chances of reaching your weight-loss goals will increase significantly.

- **You Won't Forget:** According to a study published in the *Science Daily* journal, writing your goals down on paper stimulates the hippocampus, which is the part of the brain responsible for memory. I found this to be true because when I wrote out the plan for my book, I would randomly think about it throughout the day. On the other hand, when I didn't have a plan, the thought of writing my book rarely entered my mind because I was too consumed with other stuff that wasn't even important.

- **Boosts Your Confidence:** Research suggests that people who set goals for themselves are more confident than those who don't. This is another theory I can testify to because my confidence increased as soon as I got serious about my goals. Setting goals alone doesn't boost your confidence, but working on them and seeing progress does. When I completed my first 30-day challenge and I had written 15,000 words of my book, I knew I could achieve anything I put my mind to. I was happier, and for the first time in my life, I felt like I was capable of being more than just a bystander in the world.

- **Reduces Stress and Anxiety:** Planning prevents time-wasting and boosts productivity. When you know what you need to do, you're not sitting around scratching your head trying to figure stuff out—you just get on with it. But when you don't have a plan, you end up feeling stressed and anxious because you don't know where to start and you have no control over your situation.

- **Guides You to Success:** A plan is like a compass that guides you to success. A good plan improves decision-making because you're not just throwing things out there and seeing what works. You have a strategy that you're focused on, which makes the journey to your destination a lot easier.

I became a lot more focused when I created a plan to write my book. Once I knew exactly what I needed to do and how I was going to do it, it was on and popping from there!

Other People's Opinions: The first time I decided to start writing my book, I was so excited, and I told all my friends. But they didn't give me one bit of encouragement; in fact, they laughed at me and told me there was no way I could do it. They were so confident that they placed a bet that I would give up within six months. I am well aware that their opinions of me were my fault because I was renowned for starting projects and never finishing them. We were all like that, and it was a running joke amongst us that we were just a bunch of clowns reaching for imaginary stars. Nevertheless, it still hurt that my friends didn't believe in me—and because they didn't believe in me, *I* didn't believe in me.

Your Environment: A messy or noisy environment will completely sap your motivation. Clutter is a form of distraction because it's a visual reminder that you need to tidy up, even if you don't intend on doing so. Sometimes, you'll use the clutter as an excuse not to work on your goals and start tidying up the moment you sit down to start working on your tasks. Trust me, I know—I used to do this all the time. But the joke was that I hated cleaning and I was using it as an excuse not to work on my book. Guys, please hear me when I tell you that if you don't set your environment up for success, your mind will talk you out of it. Humans don't like hard work; we are always looking for an easy way out—which is why, when I had the choice between folding laundry or writing my book, I chose folding laundry, despite the fact that I hate doing it. To me, that was the easier option. Get everything in order before you start working. If you live with people and your house is too noisy, go to the library or a coffee shop. Do whatever you need to do to get the job done.

Too Much to Do: When I first started figuring this stuff out, I really thought I was being organized by writing a to-do list before I went to bed. While writing a to-do list is a great way to keep on top of things, you defeat the purpose of the strategy when the list is too long. The next morning, I would look at the list and get completely demotivated at the thought of all the things I needed to do. Avoid this by putting a maximum of three tasks on your to-do list. When I implemented this, there were very few days when I didn't get everything done.

Diet: After stuffing my face with pizza, burgers, fries, or whatever junk food I had ordered that night, getting off the couch and working was the last thing on my mind, and so I remained on the couch for the rest of the night. I didn't realize that a bad diet affected your motivation until I started eating healthy foods and noticed a significant difference in how I felt. Prior to that, the only way to I could get myself moving was to drink loads of coffee and energy drinks.

Whether we eat what we have in the fridge or swing through a drive-through, most people don't think about what they eat; they simply eat when they get hungry and keep it moving. The body converts the food we eat into energy so we can perform our daily tasks. However, the body does not process all foods in the same way. Simple carbohydrates and sugars give us a quick boost of energy because the food is instantly turned into glucose. But shortly afterwards, you experience a massive drop in energy (hence the reason I could never get off the couch after eating). Processed foods and saturated fats don't digest well, and the body is forced to work overtime, which is what causes the tiredness. If you want to stay energized and motivated, here is a list of foods to avoid:

- **White Carbohydrates:** White carbohydrates are processed grains; they are unhealthy because the bran has been stripped from them, which reduces their fiber content. When the body doesn't get enough fiber, it absorbs the carbs quicker and finds it more difficult to digest them. White carbs have also been stripped of the germ, which is full of nutrients such as antioxidants, phytochemicals, and B vitamins, all of which play a role in maintaining energy levels.

- **Breakfast Cereals:** One of the main reasons sugar addiction is so difficult to break is because it starts in childhood. I remember my mom giving me a bowl of cereal for breakfast every morning before I went to school. What my mother and most people don't know is that breakfast cereals are full of sugar and contain very little fiber. The dangerous combination of low fiber and high sugar causes a spike in insulin and blood-sugar levels. This gives you a quick boost of energy, and then you crash shortly after. Also, research suggests that, due to the addictive nature of processed sugar, you will begin to crave sugary foods, which creates an energy-depleting cycle. Another major problem is that breakfast foods such as granola bars, muffins, juices, and yogurts are packed with processed sugars but they are advertised as healthy breakfast options!

- **Energy Drinks:** Despite the fact that they're called "energy drinks," once that initial boost wears off, you end up even more drained than you were before you had the drink. So, what do you do? Grab another one—and then you become addicted to energy drinks because it becomes one big vicious cycle. I used to have a fridge full of them and guzzle them down like water. Studies have found that energy drinks reduce sleepiness and boost memory and concentration by approximately 24%. But critics state that these deceptive positive effects are due to the ridiculously large amount of caffeine and sugar in these drinks. One can contains around 10 teaspoons (52 grams) of sugar. Consuming a lot of sugar will cause a quick energy spike and then it will take a sharp drop, which is why you end up even more tired than you were before you had the drink.

Additionally, one can of energy drink contains a lot more caffeine than one cup of coffee. For example, the brand 5-hour Energy contains four times the amount of caffeine present in one cup of coffee. Which means that drinking just two cans takes you over the recommended maximum amount of 400 mg of caffeine per day. An excessive amount of caffeine causes anxiety, jitteriness and heart palpitations. It can also increase the intensity of panic attacks.

- **Low-Calorie Foods:** It's not uncommon for people on a diet to opt for the low-calorie versions of their favorite snacks. Since calorie counting is a thing, this appears to be the healthier option. The problem is that we need calories for energy, and if you don't eat enough calories, you won't have enough energy to get you through the day. Calories are required to maintain basic functions such as heartbeat, thinking, and breathing. Consistently depriving the body of calories slows down the metabolism and causes hormonal imbalances, which leaves you feeling drained. To make matters worse, not eating enough calories makes you crave food and you end up overeating at your next meal, which makes you feel sluggish.

- **Fast and Fried Foods:** That big, juicy burger you devoured at lunchtime made you want to take a nap because fast and fried foods are low in fiber and high in fat, both of which slow down the digestive process. When the body is forced to work overtime to digest food, it takes longer to release the nutrients that boost your energy. Furthermore, these foods lack the essential vitamins and minerals required for a healthy diet. Fatty foods also make you feel full too quickly and give you a feeling of lethargy.

If you want to stay energized and motivated, here is a list of foods and drinks you should be consuming regularly:

- **Water:** The body is made up of approximately 73% water, which means that when we are dehydrated, the body slows down. Even being slightly dehydrated can have a negative effect on the brain, which is why it's so important to drink a full glass of water as soon as you wake up. Failing to drink enough water throughout the day causes you to become lethargic, distracted, and irritable. If you want to slay your goals, drink at least two liters of water per day.

- **Dark Chocolate:** When people say they love chocolate, they are generally not referring to the sour, acquired taste of dark chocolate. They mean the sugar-laden milk chocolate processed type. The good news is that healthy eating doesn't require you to give up chocolate—just switch the type. Dark chocolate gives you a spectacular boost of the feel-good hormones serotonin, endorphins, and dopamine. Apart from feeling awesome after tak-

- ing your first bite, dark chocolate also contains flavanols, which improve blood supply to the brain, making it easier for you to focus on your tasks.

- **Tomatoes:** According to research, the antioxidant lycopene found in tomatoes protects the brain against free radical damage, which improves the overall health of the brain. It is important to mention that while you might enjoy sinking your teeth into a raw tomato, it's best to eat them cooked with a dash of olive oil because it improves the absorption of lycopene.

- **Avocado:** This tasty fruit improves the flexibility of our brain-cell membranes, which improves blood flow to the brain, making it easier for us to focus on important tasks.

- **Coffee:** Dopamine is affectionately known as the feel-good hormone, but it also improves our focus and plays an important role in action-planning—both of which are essential for goal achievement. One of the many health benefits of coffee is that it increases dopamine levels in the brain, helping us to work more efficiently. You will often hear experts say that coffee is unhealthy. This is correct, but only when consumed in excess. Therefore, drink a maximum of 400 mg of caffeine per day, which is approximately four cups of coffee.

- **Pumpkin Seeds:** Before you start your day, chow down some pumpkin seeds. A small handful provides all the zinc you will need for the day. Zinc improves your thinking skills and memory, making your more alert and prepared to complete your tasks.

- **Eggplant:** Stop peeling the skin off your eggplants! The skin contains nasunin, a nutrient responsible for improving communication between the brain cells.

- **Walnuts:** Walnuts contain omega-3 fatty acids, which are known to fuel the brain. They are also known to boost serotonin levels, which helps to improve low moods.

- **Strawberries:** Research suggests that consuming a few servings of strawberries per day improves memory function. This is because strawberries contain the flavonoid fisetin, which helps create signaling pathways in the brain.

- **Kale:** The manganese in kale increases brain function and concentration. Kale is also rich in amino acids, which help to improve low moods and increase alertness.

- **Grass-Fed Beef:** As well as being low in calories and free from harmful hormones and antibiotics, grass-fed beef is high in iron, which plays an important role in motivation. A study published in *The American Journal of Clinical Nutrition* found that iron levels affected performance on mental tasks. The women in the study with low iron levels were slower than the participants with higher iron levels when it came to performing mental tasks.

- **Green Tea:** One of the many benefits of green tea is that it helps you relax. Because it contains a small amount of caffeine, it gives you that edge but it's nowhere near as intense as a cup of coffee. But green tea also contains catechins, which let your body know when it's time to take a break. This combination gives you a steady, long-lasting burst of concentration and focus.

- **Flaxseed:** Add flaxseed to your oatmeal, pancake batter, or smoothie and expect to receive a huge boost in motivation. Flaxseed is rich in alpha-linoleic acid (ALA), a healthy fat that increases the amount of glucose provided to the brain cells.

- **Greek Yogurt:** Greek yogurt is a rich source of probiotics, calcium, and protein, all of which are gut-friendly nutrients. Studies have found a strong connection between a healthy gut and brain health. In other words, the healthier your gut, the healthier your brain.

- **Sunflower Seeds:** Insomnia and depression are two of the biggest obstacles in terms of motivation. The good news is that a handful of sunflower seeds will help you fight these problems naturally. These miniscule seeds are packed with the amino acid tryptophan, which converts into serotonin once it enters the body. Serotonin is a feel-good hormone that acts as a natural mood stabilizer. It also improves sleep by triggering the release of the sleep hormone melatonin.

- **Pecans:** For those wanting to combat post-workout fatigue, depression, and memory loss, pecans are an effective choice. Pecans are rich in the essential nutrient choline, which is known to improve brain function.

- **Blueberries:** If you want to improve your engagement and focus, make blueberries a regular addition to your meals. One study found that participants who ate one cup of blueberries a day for two weeks achieved much higher grades on a test than the participants who did not eat blueberries. The researchers concluded that one reason for this was that blueberries increase brain cells in the hippocampus, the part of the brain responsible for memory.

- **Whole Grains:** Not only do these complex carbohydrates boost energy; they are rich in the B vitamin folate, which increases blood flow to the brain and improves mental processing.

- **Spinach:** Eating spinach keeps the brain healthy by protecting it against oxidative stress. Spinach makes the brain more responsive due to its potassium levels. Additionally, spinach is high in lutein, which boosts memory, learning, and overall brain function.

- **Tuna:** One serving of tuna contains 69% of your recommended daily dose of vitamin B6. A Japanese study found that participants with a vitamin B6 deficiency had low moods. When you've got the blues, the only thing you'll have the motivation to do is climb under the covers and sleep. Additionally, vitamin B6 is a popular treatment for Attention Deficit Hyperactivity Disorder (ADHD) because it is known to boost a person's ability to focus.

Okay, awesome! I've provided you with a list of healthy foods to eat and unhealthy foods to avoid. But let me warn you that changing your diet is going to be a very difficult journey. One conversation society is not having enough is about food addiction. It only becomes a problem when it's an extreme case and an obese person is forced to make an appearance on a program like *My 600-lb Life* so they can get gastric-bypass surgery.

DISCLAIMER: I am about to make two very bold claims that have not been scientifically proven. First, I believe that the majority of people in America are food-addicted. And second, I believe that food addiction is the hardest addiction to break. Why? Because it's a socially acceptable addiction. I want you to think about this for a moment. Last night you decided you were going to change your eating habits and cut out processed sugar. In the morning, you go to the store, and in front of you are hundreds of candy bars and other types of sweet treats. You know what you promised yourself last night, but the temptation is too strong and you can't resist, so you pick up a couple of candy bars and promise yourself you'll start again tomorrow. But you keep running into temptation and eventually, you just give up altogether on trying to maintain a healthy lifestyle.

Now, the government is well aware that an unhealthy diet is responsible for chronic disease such as cancer, heart disease, and diabetes. They are also aware that the majority of deaths in the United States are caused by an unhealthy diet because, according to the Centers for Disease Control and Prevention, heart attack has been the leading cause of death in America since 1950. With this knowledge, wouldn't it be wise to remove all unhealthy foods and beverages from the supermarket shelves? A drug addict doesn't have such easy access to their drug of choice because it's illegal. Imagine if they could just walk into a store and buy it over the counter. There would be uproar in the country. But the person addicted to food is faced with the temptation of their "drug" of choice each time they walk into a store. Food addiction is a socially acceptable form of suicide. I do not believe there is one adult in America who does not know that an unhealthy diet kills—yet no one bats an eyelid when we're all crammed into McDonald's shoving burgers down our throats. However, I am certain that many people would call the police if they witnessed someone taking illegal drugs in a public place.

It took me over two years to beat my food addiction. I'm an all-or-nothing person; I wasn't doing the "treat yourself every once in a while" strategy because that doesn't work for me. That treat would always turn into a month-long binge of unhealthy eating, which would set me back mentally and physically. However you want to implement your healthy-eating plan is up to you; I'm just giving you a heads-up about how hard it's going to be. You will need an extreme amount of willpower to beat a food addiction.

What to Do When You Have No Motivation

Some mental health experts argue that having no motivation is a symptom of a bigger problem such as depression, self-doubt, or the avoidance of discomfort. If you feel there is an underlying reason as to why you lack motivation, please seek professional help. However, in general, it can be normal to have no motivation—but remember, motivation is an emotion, and you can tap into it when you want to. Here are some tips:

Ten-Minute Intervals: Working in ten-minute intervals is a great way to get started when you have no motivation because it's not such a shock to the brain. There were days when I couldn't be bothered to get out of bed, or I had got too comfortable on the sofa. If I had a goal in mind of writing 1000 words and I tried to convince myself that it was "only 1000 words," it never worked because I know how long it takes to write 1000 words. The thought of writing for an hour or more shut me down mentally. However, when I told myself that I was "only going to write for 10 minutes," I got up and got to work. I would set an alarm for 10 minutes, but when it went off, most of the time I had already got into flow mode and I'd turn it off and carry on writing. So, whatever you've got to do, trick your mind into thinking you're only going to be doing it for 10 minutes. If you keep working past the 10 minutes, great, but if not, that's fine too because at least you did something.

Listen to Music: It has been proven by science that music raises morale, improves focus, makes you more confident and makes you happier. A 2019 study reported by the *PNAS Journal* found that when getting ready for an important presentation or trying to get familiar with a pile of paperwork before a meeting, music triggers the brain's reward system, motivating you to get in the zone and absorb information. What music you choose to listen to is up to you—just make sure it has that motivational effect.

Listen to a Motivational Speech: There are many people online sharing their stories of success who endured insurmountable challenges in order to be who they are today. Nick Vujicic, for example, is an Australian-American evangelist, author, and motivational speaker who was born with no arms and legs. Nick chose not to allow his disabilities to define him, and he has achieved more with no limbs than most able-bodied people have in their lifetime. Listening to someone like him puts things in perspective, which can motivate you to get moving.

Give Yourself a Reward: Rewards are effective because of the psychological component associated with them. The feel-good hormone dopamine increases in the brain when we become aware of a reward. This feeling is addictive, and the mind and body begin to crave it. When people hear the word *addiction*, they automatically think of the negative aspects of it, which are typically drug- and alcohol-related. However, addiction is extremely beneficial when it encourages positive behaviors. Becoming dependent on rewards trains the mind to view hard work as related to a reward. There are several benefits associated with rewarding yourself. Here are some of them:

- **You Develop Good Habits:** Working hard for a reward will soon become a habit, which means it will become a lot easier for you to achieve your goals.

- **Fewer Distractions:** When you reward yourself with the things you enjoy the most, you'll be able to eliminate distractions more easily. When you feel tempted to pick up your phone and scroll through social media, your mind will immediately give you a choice: Instagram or reward? Since you value the reward more, you will choose the reward.

- **Increased Focus:** Rewards give you clarity of mind and tunnel vision. Whatever it is you need to do will become your main focus. And it won't be a one-time event; eventually, you will start every workday with this intense level of focus.

- **Less Procrastination:** Completing tasks on your to-do list is addictive, making the reward system a powerful way to get you through the work week. When you know you've got a treat waiting for you once you finish your projects, you'll have an extra dose of motivation to work harder.

Rewarding yourself doesn't need to be anything fancy. In case you are wondering how to reward yourself after completing a project or a hard day's work, here are some tips:

- Take a trip to your favorite coffee shop and purchase the most extravagant cup of coffee on the menu.
- Listen to an entire playlist of your favorite tracks.
- Buy yourself something new.
- If you have any holiday days left, take a day off work and relax.
- Spend the evening watching Netflix.
- Visit the museum, theater, or go and see a sporting event.
- Spend time with someone you care about.
- Go to a workout class you haven't tried before.
- Order a takeout or go to your favorite restaurant.
- Don't set an alarm—sleep until you wake up.
- Eat some ice cream or chocolate.
- Enjoy a hot shower or a bubble bath.
- Start reading a book.

These rewards are just suggestions; everyone has their own personal tastes, so do whatever will make you happy.

Think About Your *Why*: Think about what you want to achieve and why. Maybe you desire to start your own business to have the financial freedom to travel. Or you want to put your children through private school. Whatever your reason for wanting to achieve your goals, the next time you don't feel motivated, spend a couple of minutes thinking about it. If your *why* is strong enough, you will get to work.

Think of the Negative Consequences: Les Brown said something during one of his speeches that shook me to my core. He said:

> *"Imagine what it will be like at the end of your days. You are lying in bed during the last minute of your life, and instead of your family surrounding your bedside lovingly saying goodbye, you are surrounded by your unfulfilled dreams. They are angry and frustrated and they scream at you, saying, 'Why didn't you give us life? Why weren't you brave enough to turn us into a reality? You are so selfish, because no one else can give us life except for you, and now we are going to die with you.'"*

It sounds extreme, but that is what will happen if you don't achieve your goals. Obviously, your dreams are not going to shout at you on your deathbed, but you will regret not achieving them. You will go to your grave with that nagging feeling of *what if*. I believe that everyone was created to do something specific on earth. The thing that *I* was created to do, *you* can't do, and the thing that *you* were created to do, *I* can't do. We all have a unique calling.

I've always had this thought that if we don't complete our assignment on earth, when we die, we will go to a movie theater and watch the story of our lives. The film will show us who we could have become, and what we could have achieved if we had achieved our goals. I don't know about you, but I never want to see that movie! As my friend Mr. Hamilton said, when we die, there will be a date on either side of the dash: the date you were born, and the date you died. What you do in between those dates is up to you. Choose wisely.

Okay, so, once you psych yourself up to get to work, and you achieve your goal, it's not about stopping there. Success is not a onetime event; it's a lifestyle. And in order to make it a lifestyle, you need self-discipline. Read all about it in Chapter 9.

CHAPTER 9:

DEVELOPING DISCIPLINE: NOTHING HAPPENS WITHOUT SELF-DISCIPLINE

> *"We all have dreams. But in order to make dreams come into reality, it takes an awful lot of determination, dedication, self-discipline, and effort."*
> ~Jesse Owens

You can be the most talented person in the world, but if you have no self-discipline, you will never be successful. I used to believe that success was about luck until I learned that success was about your habits and self-discipline. Roman philosopher Seneca said, "Luck is what happens when preparation meets opportunity." In order to prepare, you must be disciplined. When we turn on the TV or open a magazine and get exposed to the glitz and glamor, some of us assume that the rich and famous just got picked out of the crowd and became successful. Or we assume it's because of their looks, or because they have contacts in the industry. But most of these people were training hard behind the scenes before making their first appearances on screen. Take Venus and Serena Williams, for example; they trained for four years, six hours a day, six days a week before anyone recognized their hard work and dedication. Self-discipline is the main character in the show—without it, nothing happens.

What Is Self-Discipline?

According to the *Collins Dictionary*, self-discipline is "The ability to make yourself work hard or behave in a particular way without needing anyone else to tell you what to do." After I became successful, an old friend (I'll call him Jack) contacted me and wanted to know how I did it. We were work colleagues, and on our lunch breaks we would sit and talk about how much we hated our jobs. When we spoke on the phone, that was all we talked about—how much we hated our jobs and what we wished we could be doing instead. He was one of the people I had to cut off (more on that later) when I started getting serious about achieving my goals because I was trying to change my mindset, and he wasn't ready to make the shift yet. Anyway, I don't have anything against the guy, so when he called, I spoke to him. He explained that he was ready to get this show on the road and follow my path to success. I told him what to do, gave him some books to read, and recommended seminars to attend.

We hung up the phone, and a week later he called again, this time asking me to write out a program for him to follow because he'd tried to get through all the material I gave him but he just couldn't seem to figure it out. When I asked him how many chapters of each book he had read, it turned out that he'd skimmed through all of them but had only read two chapters because he's not much of a reader. "Okay, get the audiobooks then, and listen to them on your way to work," I advised. I told him I would not be creating a program for him and that he needed to read the books for himself. The next week, he called back saying it was taking him too long to listen to the audiobooks and could I just create a program for him? I said no, and he never called back. The last I heard he was running around town telling people I thought I was too good for everyone because I wouldn't help him out.

As far as I was concerned, I *did* help him. I gave him all the materials he needed to succeed—if he was willing to put the work in. But like most people, he was looking for a shortcut to success. Jack didn't want to do what I had done to get to my level; he wanted me to pull him up. Jack didn't read the books because he had no self-discipline. He didn't want to read the books, or attend the seminars. However, as mentioned, self-discipline is about doing the things you don't want to do. When we worked together, Jack and I were exactly the same. When we spoke on the phone, we were both doing the same thing—scrolling through social media and eating junk food. Jack wanted me to give him what it had taken me over two years to develop. To achieve my goals, I had to develop self-discipline, and so will anyone else. Maybe learning about the benefits of self-discipline will convince you.

WHAT ARE THE BENEFITS OF SELF-DISCIPLINE?

Self-discipline is the foundation of success in all areas of your life. If you are going to achieve anything, you will need self-discipline. Here are some of its main benefits:

Improved Relationships: While this is never spoken about, one of the main reasons relationships break down is a lack of self-discipline. A study conducted by Vrije University in Amsterdam found that those with high levels of self-control are considered more trustworthy. People in relationships with no self-control are more likely to cheat, not keep their promises, and say things they shouldn't. All these things significantly contribute to failed relationships. On the other hand, those with self-discipline achieve their goals, do what they say they are going to do, and remain calm during disagreements. Additionally, it's important to understand that relationships are hard work. Hollywood has lied to us and tricked us into believing that when you meet your significant other, you'll fall head over heels in love, ride off into the sunset together and live happily ever after. Well, that's clearly not the case, considering over 50% of marriages end in divorce. Why? Because in many cases, people don't have the self-discipline to do the work necessary to fix the relationship.

Less Anxiety and Stress: How do you feel when a deadline is looming and you haven't even started the project? Anxious and stressed-out, right? You can prevent this by completing the project before the deadline. By getting started on it as soon as it's assigned to you, managing your time and working on it daily. However, it takes self-discipline to achieve this because when you know you've got time to do it, you procrastinate. Every day, you say you'll do it tomorrow until there are no tomorrows left. This phenomenon is referred to as "Parkinson's Law," a term coined in 1955 by British historian and author Cyril Northcote Parkinson. According to this law, the more time you have to complete a project, the more difficult it becomes to complete it. For example, you could have a task to do that you know is only going to take one hour to complete. However, instead of getting it done straight away, you give yourself a one-week deadline.

Initially, you feel relieved that you have more than enough time to complete the project, but that relief quickly turns into stress and anxiety when you leave it to the last minute.

Guaranteed Success: According to Theodore Roosevelt, "With self-discipline, almost anything is possible." The bottom line is that nobody is going to achieve your goals on your behalf—*you* are the only person capable of turning your dreams into reality. Success is not an easy ride; the work you will need to do to become successful requires an extreme amount of discipline. You have to fight with yourself every day to do the right thing—to get up early instead of hitting the snooze button, to work rather than play computer games, or to work instead of scrolling through social media—these are choices only you can make. Additionally, there is no smooth road to success; many obstacles will show up along the way. With self-discipline, you can plow through them instead of giving up.

Control Over Your Life: One of the main reasons people feel as if they have no control over their life is a lack of self-discipline. I know *I* felt this way. As mentioned, at the beginning of every year, I set a goal to write my book, but I could never do it because I didn't have the right systems in place. I didn't know I was failing because I had no self-discipline. I assumed success just wasn't for me; there was only a handful of people destined for greatness and I wasn't one of them. Everything in my life was a mess because that was what I had created. I rolled out of bed with just enough time to get to work by 9:00 a.m., never even making my bed. My house was always a mess, so I could never find anything. The TV was always on, and I was always speaking on the phone or scrolling through social media. I could go on, but I think you get my point. There was no order in my life and it affected my ability to be productive. Things only started coming together for me when I became more self-disciplined.

Your Confidence Improves: A lack of self-discipline will completely destroy your confidence. As the days and months go by without you achieving anything, you will feel more and more worthless. You will try and limit this feeling of worthlessness by blaming other people for your failure. I blamed my parents for not being rich enough to give me the money I needed to quit my 9–5 job so I could write my book. I blamed by friends for calling me too much and distracting me, and I blamed society for creating a system called capitalism. I had so many excuses for my failure, it was ridiculous. However, deep down, I knew *I* was the only person who could change things. It was up to me and no one else. When I decided to make this work and write 500 words a day for 30 days, I noticed a massive increase in my confidence after those 30 days. The progress I had made during that time made me realize I could do this. The more chapters I wrote, the more confident I became.

Your Mental Strength Improves: Self-discipline is a battle with the mind, and those who lack self-discipline simply don't have the mental fortitude to say no to immediate gratification. The good news is that this state of mind is not permanent—you can change it. According to neuroscientists, our habits are encrypted in our brain by deep-rooted neural pathways. However, the brain is a lot more malleable than formerly believed. The brain is similar to plastic, and it can be molded as such. The neural pathways that drive bad habits can be overridden with new neural pathways that guide good habits. For example, let's say a person has a bad habit of self-medicating with food or alcohol when they feel stressed. If they have a desire to change this bad habit, they can override it with a good habit such as exercise. The more they do this, the stronger the new neural pathways will become until eventually, the bad habit of eating and drinking alcohol during times of stress will be replaced by exercise. In the beginning, this will be extremely difficult and will take a lot of willpower to achieve—but eventually, you will get there.

Although I have yet to have a brain scan to determine whether this theory is correct, I believe I have experienced it personally. When I first decided to wake up half an hour earlier and write for 30 minutes, I struggled immensely. I had to disrupt my normal routine of hitting the snooze button multiple times, or picking up my phone to check my messages or social media. It took everything in me to fight this battle, and I failed several times before I became consistent. One of the things I did to help me was buy a regular alarm clock and leave my phone in the car overnight. It sounds extreme, but it worked. It took way more effort to go outside and get my phone (especially when it was cold) than to sit down and write for 30 minutes. Initially, the first thing I thought about when I woke up was my phone, but after a few weeks, the first thing I thought about when I woke up was writing my book. And that's what I did—went straight to the computer. That habit has not changed.

How to Develop Self-Discipline

The good news is that anyone can develop self-discipline. My life is a testament to this. However, it's not going to happen overnight. There is no magical self-discipline pill you can take. I'm sorry to sound harsh, but if you're not prepared to do the work, you might as well shut this book now! But if you *are* ready to develop extraordinary self-discipline, keep reading. First, though, so you don't get overwhelmed, here's some info on why self-discipline is so difficult.

Have you ever felt like you are two people in one—the good version of you, and the bad version? When you want to do the things that will improve your life, the bad version of you will encourage you to do the wrong thing. And nine times out of ten, guess who wins? The bad version of you. It's extremely frustrating and exhausting, to say the least. This is the reason self-discipline is so difficult—because we are fighting with ourselves and using force to control our thoughts and behavior. Using force for anything never works. It may work over the short term, but not over the long term. So, what's the solution if mentally beating yourself into submission isn't? It starts with mindfulness.

Practice Mindfulness: When we become obsessed with choices, good or bad, right or wrong, we fall into the self-improvement trap instead of building self-discipline. Mindfulness is a practice that teaches you how to focus on the present moment, and self-discipline is all about the present moment. For example, let's say you want to change your diet and you get a craving to order a takeout. Instead of forcing yourself not to think about the craving and eat something healthier, take note of the craving and then do something else. Research suggests that taking a brisk walk for 15 minutes can help beat sugary cravings. If it's too late to go for a walk, get on YouTube and follow a short home workout. Additionally, chewing gum can help reduce junk-food cravings. Or you could be working on a project and you get the urge to check social media. Again, don't try and deny the urge—acknowledge it, and do something else. The mind often goes to social media when it needs a distraction. Needing a break away from what you are doing is not the problem; the problem is what you *do* during the break. Instead of reaching for your phone, pick up a book, go and get a glass of water, or make yourself a sandwich. If you play a musical instrument, play on it for a few minutes and then get back to work.

Figure Out What Works: Figuring out what does and does not work for you is essential to becoming more disciplined. Some people work very well with others around, while others prefer working alone. For some, rewards are a great motivator; for others, the consequences of not getting it done is enough. This is known as "carrot versus stick." Start by answering these questions to help you become more disciplined:

- Am I more distracted when I am around people, or does it help me concentrate?

- Do I work best in the house or in the library/co-working space?

- Am I motivated by the thought of a reward after completing a task?

- Does the thought of taking away a treat or a privilege for not getting something done motivate me?

- Does thinking about the bigger picture encourage me more than visualizing small steps?

- What are the things that are hindering me the most from becoming more disciplined?

- What are the things that are stopping me from achieving my goals?

Once you've answered these questions, you'll have a better understanding of the approach you need to take in order to become more disciplined.

Find an Accountability Partner: Trying to do this on your own can be extremely difficult, and if you can find an accountability partner, I would advise that you get one. An accountability partner is someone who works with you to ensure you meet your targets. If they catch you slipping, they will pull you up on it. This could be a friend or a relative—just make sure they have the same mindset as you or there's a high chance they'll fail at holding you accountable. I didn't get an accountability partner until I was a couple of years into my journey because I didn't know anyone who was ready to walk this path. But when I finally got one, I became even more motivated to achieve my goals. Here are some of the main benefits associated with having an accountability partner:

- **They Provide Advice and Support:** In most cases, an accountability partner has been in your shoes. They are often a lot more successful than you and know exactly what you need to do in order to achieve your goals. They know what mistakes you need to avoid, and when you are struggling, they can help you see things from a different perspective. An accountability partner can also identify your strengths and weaknesses and give you insight into the areas where you need to make improvements.

- **They Are Happy for You:** Unfortunately, as you'll discover in Chapter 11, many of your friends will not support your decision to become more than what you currently are, and they will not be happy for you when you achieve your goals. However, an accountability partner will cheer you along because they want to see you win. They will have seen where you started from and will be proud of the progress you've made.

- **They Keep You Motivated:** The road to success is a very lonely journey, and having someone there to cheer you on can be very helpful. There will be days when you'll feel as if you can't take another step. When you are so tired you want to give up. Sometimes, it's just too difficult to motivate yourself because the only energy you have is to stay in bed. But when you have an accountability partner, they can give you the motivation you can't give yourself. They can remind you why you started and why it's so important to finish.

Start Small: For most people, trying to do too much at once always ends in disaster because the subconscious mind simply can't comprehend such a leap and it will do everything in its power to get you back in your comfort zone. For example, let's say your goal is to lose weight through healthy eating and exercise. You get really excited about it and create a plan to help you shed those pounds. Your plan involves eating only fruits and vegetables for 60 days, and doing two hours of cardio per day. As far as you're concerned, this is the perfect plan for you and you get very excited envisioning your new trim body. You manage to keep it up for three days, then on the fourth day, you hit the snooze button and tell yourself you'll do one hour of cardio instead of two, which you do. Then for lunch, you decide to throw in one slice of bread with your salad, and for dinner, you add a plate of spaghetti to your vegetables. It's downhill from that day forward. What happened was that your brain couldn't handle such a dramatic shift and it forced you back into your old habits. Once you'd reverted to what you knew, you gave up completely because you decided that achieving your goal was impossible.

There are very few people who can take on such a challenge and accomplish it because it takes an abnormal amount of willpower to achieve. If that's the direction you want to take, then go ahead. However, achieving your goals is much easier when you take small steps. It will take longer, but it won't be so difficult because your brain won't find the adjustment so abnormal, and it will slowly get used to what you are doing. So, instead of going so hard, you would give yourself six months to lose the weight. Instead of doing such an extreme diet, you could go on the ketogenic diet where you cut out carbohydrates but you can still eat meat and lots of other yummy treats. With a diet like this, you won't feel as if you're restricting yourself so much. For exercise, you could go for a 15-minute jog every morning. You are more likely to keep up with a routine like this because it doesn't seem so overwhelming. So, whatever goal you've set for yourself, start small. Once you begin making progress and your body starts getting used to the changes, you can work your way up by increasing the time you jog to 20 minutes and cutting out more unhealthy foods.

Remove Your Weaknesses: Oscar Wilde once said, "I can resist anything except temptation." In other words, when the temptation is right in front of you, you are more likely to give in to it. When I decided to start taking care of my health and ditch junk food, I had a pantry full of snacks and a fridge full of sodas that I didn't want to get rid of. I believed I could override the temptation to eat them, but it was impossible. I made the excuse that I was keeping them for guests because I didn't want to waste food. However, every time I got a craving for something sweet (which was practically every day) guess what I did? I stuffed my face and said I would start again tomorrow. This continued until I had eaten all the snacks and drunk all the soda. It was at that point that I filled my fridge with healthy drinks and snacks. However, what I should have done if I was so concerned with wasting food is give it away. I could have given it to friends or food banks, but the reality is that I wasn't ready to give up junk food, and I wanted to eat what I had left.

The same applied to my TV. My snacks and television went hand in hand. I would lie on the sofa stuffing my face with snacks while watching TV. The situation was always the same—I would tell myself I was only going to have one bag of chips and one soda while watching one of my favorite programs. That never happened; I always ended up watching at least three TV programs, eating several bags of chips, and drinking several cans of soda. Most nights, I would fall asleep on the couch. I tried so hard to resist the temptation to watch television, but it never worked. I had to take extreme measures and sell the TV. To this day, I still don't have a TV in my house, and nor do I keep unhealthy snacks in the fridge because you will be surprised at how easy it is to fall back into bad habits when the temptation is present. The best way to deal with temptation is to get rid of it.

Start a Daily Routine: Consistency is key when it comes to changing your habits; therefore, the most effective way to build discipline is to have a daily routine. The most successful people in the world say that one of the secrets to their success is a strict daily routine. Let's take a look at some of their daily routines:

Sir Richard Branson: He is the founder of the Virgin Group. According to *Forbes*, he is worth $3.6 billion, making him the 798th richest person in the world. Branson has over 40 million social media followers, and he blogs about issues ranging from the importance of fulfilling your life's purpose, adventure, and environment, to entrepreneurship.

- Wakes up at 5:00 a.m.
- Exercises
- Eats breakfast
- Spends time with family
- Gets to work

Oprah Winfrey: The American television personality and media mogul Oprah Winfrey is one of the most influential women in the United States. She shot to fame with her daytime talk show *The Oprah Winfrey Show*. She is the founder of the Oprah Winfrey Network and is worth $2.8 billion.

- Wakes up at 7:10 a.m.
- Takes the dogs out for a walk
- Has a cup of coffee
- Reads an inspirational card from her 365 Gathered Truths Box
- Reads something from *The Bowl of Saki*
- Meditates for 20 minutes
- Works out for one hour
- Gets to work

Tim Cook: Tim Cook is the CEO of Apple, one of the world's most influential and valuable technology companies. Cook joined Apple in 1998 and played a crucial role in the company's success. He is also known for his advocacy for LGBTQ rights.

- Wakes up at 4:00 a.m.
- Reads feedback emails from customers
- Goes to the gym
- Eats breakfast
- Gets to work

Michelle Obama: Michelle Obama is the wife of the former president of the United States Barack Obama. She is a lawyer and a writer, and was the first African-American First Lady of the United States.

- Wakes up at 4:30 a.m.
- Drinks coffee
- Works out
- Has breakfast
- Gets to work

Successful people have several things in common. They all wake up early, and they all exercise. Why is this?

According to biology professor Chris Randler, early birds have better business acumen. Randler's research found that early risers do better in school, which gets them into the best colleges and opens the door to better job opportunities. He also discovered that early risers are more proactive because they foresee problems and do the work required to minimize them.

In theory, this makes sense because the brain is rested in the morning, which boosts your motivation and makes you less distracted. Although people are more creative at night, they are more productive in the morning. This might be why those who wake up early are promoted often and get the best-paying jobs.

Additionally, early risers are less likely to procrastinate. A study conducted in 1997 by psychologist Joseph Ferrari discovered that procrastinators referred to themselves as "night people," and that the longer they stayed up in the evening, the more they procrastinated. Ferrari conducted the same study in 2008, and the results were the same: those who stay awake late avoid important tasks throughout the day. Furthermore, research suggests that procrastinators put their careers in jeopardy when they wait until the last minute to get stuff done.

Everyone knows that exercise has several health benefits, but what most people don't know is that it boosts productivity. Research suggests that exercise makes us smarter, more energetic, and happier, all of which help us become more productive. Here are some of the main reasons this is true:

Improves Concentration: Exercise feeds the brain by keeping your oxygen, blood, and glucose levels high, all of which are required so the brain can focus on the task at hand. Additionally, exercise plays a role in stimulating brain plasticity and new healthy connections in the brain cells. The more focused you are, the easier it is to do the things you need to do to achieve your goals.

Improves Memory: When we exercise, the muscles produce a hormone called irisin, and when it enters the brain, it improves cognition. Studies also show that exercise triggers the growth of new neurons in the brain's memory center. The more neurons the brain's memory center has, the sharper your memory becomes.

Improves Mental Stamina: Mental stamina is essential when it comes to productivity, and exercise helps to build it. When you're sleeping better during the night and you have more energy throughout the day, your mental stamina improves. You will have more resilience, which will enable you to cope with life's challenges more effectively.

Boosts Creativity: According to a 2013 study, our body and our creative mind are connected. This connection grows even deeper through regular exercise. Another study found that active people come up with better ideas than those who live a sedentary lifestyle. Additionally, regular exercise boosts the production of new brain cells, which sharpens the mind.

Boosts Energy: Exercise triggers the growth of mitochondria. Mitochondria are the structures within our cells that create an energy-boosting chemical called ATP. Productivity increases when you have more energy because you are more alert and focused, meaning you can get more done.

Improves Mood: Exercise stimulates the release of feel-good hormones such as dopamine. When you feel good, you're more likely to want to work because you have a more optimistic outlook on life.

Fights Fatigue: There's not much you can do when you're so tired you can't keep your eyes open. However, research suggests that regular exercise boosts energy levels and fights fatigue.

Exercise stimulates the release of endorphins, which increases oxygen levels in the blood and makes you feel more energized. Moderate aerobic exercise can increase the amount of slow-wave or deep sleep that a person gets. When the body and brain are rested and rejuvenated, it results in less fatigue.

Exercises to Boost Productivity

If you're not sure where to start with your exercise routine, here are a few exercises that will help boost your productivity:

Mindful Yoga: A study published in *The Journal of Physiological Sciences* found that as little as 15 minutes of focusing on your breathing makes you less stressed and more relaxed and focused, which ultimately helps to boost your productivity.

Low-Intensity Aerobic Exercises: Low-intensity exercises are just as effective as high-intensity exercises. Low-intensity aerobic exercises include step aerobics, swimming, rowing, and jogging, all of which get the heart rate up. Despite the gentleness of these exercises, when done consistently, they will improve your health and fitness levels, which will in turn boost your mental faculties and productivity levels.

Strength Training: Sit-ups, squats, push-ups, resistance bands, lifting weights, hill walking, cycling, and stair climbing are all strength-training exercises. Strength training exercises help to boost productivity because they make you more alert. Getting the heart rate up increases blood flow to the brain, which sharpens your awareness. When you feel more awake and alert, you are going to be more productive.

The Benefits of a Daily Routine

Oftentimes, when people hear the word "routine," they associate it with repetitive, rote, boring. But as all successful people know, routines are extremely powerful. Whatever you want out of life, whether it's to boost your productivity, improve your health, or make more money, a consistent daily routine will help you achieve this. There are several benefits to having a daily routine. Here are some of them:

Intentional Living: Most people just live their lives from day to day without considering the future. Even if they have goals, those goals are rarely achieved because they've always got one hundred and ten other things to take care of. But most of the time, these things are not important—they are simply distractions. When there is no order in your life, it becomes impossible to achieve anything because you're constantly fighting through chaos and barely have space in your brain to even *think* about achieving your goals. However, when you have a daily routine, your life becomes intentional. You will get into the habit of waking up at a certain time, and doing the things you need to do in the morning to ensure your goals are achieved. As you start seeing progress, it will motivate you to continue. As you keep repeating the same steps every day, eventually your daily routine will become a normal part of your life, and so will achieving your goals.

Less Stress and Anxiety: How do you feel every morning when you're running out of the house with not a minute to spare? You can't find your keys or your wallet, and you know there's something else you need, but you can't quite put your finger on it—until you're 10 minutes away from your house.

Then you've got to make a sharp U-turn to go back home and collect it! A daily routine makes you a lot more organized and less forgetful. I can strongly identify with this. Until I developed a daily routine, I was always losing things and always late because I couldn't find anything. I desperately needed a cleaning routine because my apartment was always a mess. And so every evening, when I got back from work, the first thing I did was spend half an hour cleaning. My apartment wasn't spotless, but everything was where it was supposed to be, and I felt a lot more in control of my environment. My apartment was so untidy that I felt embarrassed when a friend or family member turned up unexpectedly and I would have to scoop laundry off the chairs so the person would have somewhere to sit. I was constantly in a state of panic because my life was all over the place. I saw an immediate difference once I got into a solid routine.

Boosts Productivity and Creativity: Here's what the bestselling author Haruki Murakami said during an interview with *The Paris Review*:

> *"When I'm in writing mode for a novel, I get up at 4:00 a.m. and work for five to six hours. In the afternoon, I run for 10 kilometers or swim for 1,500 meters (or do both), then I read a bit and listen to some music. I go to bed at 9:00 p.m. I keep this routine every day without variation. The repetition itself becomes the important thing; it's a form of mesmerism. I mesmerize myself to reach a deeper state of mind."*

Of course I'm not expecting you to go this hard; this example is a bit on the extreme side because no one with a 9–5 job can have a routine like this. But the point I'm trying to make is that repetition matters. When you do the same thing over and over again, your brain becomes sharper, your output becomes higher, and your creativity is taken to another level.

You Will Have More Time: Despite the limiting beliefs I had about my craft, I love writing; it's my passion. But I had convinced myself that I didn't have time to write because my day was so disorganized and I wasted so much time doing things that didn't contribute to achieving my goals. But when I got into a routine, not a day went by that I didn't get something down on paper—well, on Word. Daily practice keeps your goals at the forefront of your mind. You'll find that whatever you're working on, you'll keep thinking about it throughout the day, and it will be the last thing you think about before you fall asleep. Repetition is a very powerful way to engage the subconscious mind. Once your subconscious mind is driving you in the direction you desire to go, there's no stopping you. Having a routine makes sure that the things you want to do are done well because, according to motivational speaker Les Brown, practice makes improvement. One of the practices I decided to include in my daily routine was meditation. When I first started, I wasn't very good at it and my mind was all over the place. But now I'm awesome at it, and I've reaped the benefits because I kept at it. The more I practice, the better I get.

How to Create a Daily Routine

It would be tempting to copy one of the daily routines of the people you read about earlier. But while they all have awesome routines, they might not be what you need. Instead, take some time to craft a daily routine that will work perfectly for *you*. Start by monitoring the things you do every day for one week.

The Power of Action

Every evening, sit down and write out step by step everything you did from the moment you woke up. This might seem like a pointless exercise, but it's actually very effective because you'll realize how much time you actually waste doing fruitless things that don't benefit you.

At the end of the week, read over everything you've done that week and pay attention to how much time you waste. Now that you've acknowledged this, I want you to write down one goal you can achieve within six months. Then write down what you would need to do every day to accomplish that goal. For example, you want to lose 40 lbs; that would mean you'll need to lose 1.5 lbs per week. That's very doable, and you wouldn't even need to work that hard. You could achieve that by cutting out white carbs and sugar, drinking more water, eating more fruit and vegetables, and going for a brisk walk every morning. Whatever it is that you need to do during those six months to achieve your goal, make sure you do it every day.

Now, write the routine out step by step. Here's what *my* first daily routine was like:

- Wake up at 5:30 a.m.
- Brush my teeth for two minutes
- Make my bed
- Drink half a liter of water
- Make a cup of coffee
- Write 500 words of my book
- Do 30 minutes on the exercise bike
- Have breakfast
- Get ready for work

I did this every day for 30 days, and then kept going until the book was written. Trust me—when you see the progress after those 30 days, you'll be so motivated and encouraged that you won't want to stop. I used to scoff at gurus who were so adamant that "it only takes 30 days to change your life." It sounds so unrealistic because 30 days is such a short amount of time. Well, it must be a magic number or something—because it works!

Implement the 40% Rule

Whatever we are doing, whether it's working out, jogging, or working on a project, most of us quit when we feel tired. But the Navy SEALs are different; they use the 40% rule to push through their mental and physical pain. According to the 40% rule, when your mind tells you it's time to give up, you have only reached 40% of your capacity, and you still have an additional 60% you can tap into. The key is to push through the resistance. It is not only the Navy SEALs who successfully use the 40% rule—many others have used it too. Marathon runners are typically known to hit the wall at 16 to 20 miles, when they feel like they don't have anything left to give. However, the majority of them finish the race, which means they found a way to tap into their reserves and force their way through the mental barrier.

You can apply the 40% rule to all areas of life including your relationships, career, and personal development. When you get to the point where you feel as if you've reached your limit and can't go any further, instead of surrendering to what your mind is telling you, remind yourself that you've got another 60% to give, and keep going. It doesn't matter what the situation is—you could be having issues in your relationship, or struggling at work. The key is to not give up when your mind tells you to, because you've got plenty more to give.

I'd love to tell you that this is easy, but it isn't, because everything in you is going to scream at you to quit. It takes discipline and mental toughness to keep pushing despite the discomfort that you feel when your mind is telling you to throw in the towel. However, the more you practice the 40% rule, the easier it will become, and you will begin to experience success in every area of your life. Here are some additional tips on how to implement the 40% rule:

- Everyone faces mental barriers. The challenges you experience are normal. The key is to recognize them and not give in to them.

- Don't try and tackle a large project at once, because when you look at it as a whole, you'll get tired very quickly. It will be a lot easier to apply the 40% rule when the project has been broken down, and you've set deadlines for each part.

- Give yourself a confidence boost by using positive self-talk. For example, when it gets hard, don't say, "This is impossible," but say, "This isn't going to be easy, but I will figure it out."

- Create a strategy or a plan to work through the challenge. For example, if you struggle with time management, create a to-do list or a schedule and prioritize your tasks.

- Set realistic expectations and goals for yourself. For example, if you are learning something new, don't expect to become an expert immediately; and don't get discouraged when you don't see progress right away.

- Don't burn yourself out—take breaks when you need to. If you are working on a project, at least once an hour, stand up, walk around, stretch, and get some fresh air. Once you feel rejuvenated, get back to work.

- Boost motivation by using visualization techniques. For example, visualize yourself achieving a goal, or completing a task. Hold that mental image in your mind and use it to motivate yourself to keep working at it.

- Keep the positive energy flowing by reading inspirational books, listening to inspirational people, and spending time with people who encourage and uplift you.

- Don't be too rigid—if a particular technique or strategy isn't working, don't be afraid to try something else that might work better for you.

At this point, if you are applying what you are reading, you should feel mentally stronger than ever. You're working on building a healthy mind, your house is in order, you've ditched the distractions, and you are practicing self-discipline. You are well on your way to greatness. However, there will be some days when you just feel stuck, and you can't seem to get moving. On those days, you'll need momentum. Keep reading to learn all about the power of momentum.

CHAPTER 10:

CREATING MOMENTUM: TAP INTO THE SNOWBALL EFFECT

"Keep moving ahead because action creates momentum, which in turn creates unanticipated opportunities."
~Nick Vujicic

In cartoons, when a snowball rolls down a hill, it starts off small and grows bigger as it collects more and more snow as it heads to the bottom. Achieving your goals works in the same way. Every year, when I made a New Year's resolution to write my book, I kept looking towards the end result. I was so obsessed with making these big changes in my life that I would set an unrealistic goal of writing the book within a couple of months. I didn't think there was any other way to do it. I wanted to make big changes, and I wanted to be perfect. But within a few weeks, I always fell flat on my face, never to recover. The all-or-nothing approach didn't work, and my desire to see quick results always ended in disaster. What I didn't understand was that consistency is the key to success, and it's one of the most powerful principles I've learned on this journey.

The Power of Consistency

> *"It's not what we do once in a while that shapes our lives, but what we do consistently."*
> —Tony Robbins.

I am the type of person who sets a goal today and wants to see it manifest tomorrow, and I think that's the case with most people. I don't like the word *consistency* because it requires patience, and I don't have much patience. But I have learned that consistency is the key to success, no matter what you want to achieve, because it creates stability. Humans need structure and stability; we want a predictable life and therefore have a strong desire for automation. When we know what's coming, we don't need to use as much energy, which means we are more likely to do the things we need to do to reach our goals. This boosts momentum and motivation to keep working on our goals.

Whatever lifestyle changes you want to make, whether it's your diet, practicing gratitude, or saving for retirement, you will need consistency to effectively implement them and for them to become permanent habits. Whatever you repeat develops into a habit, which is why successful people make success look so easy. It's the norm to them. My favorite football player is Ronaldo. He has tremendous skill with the ball and makes it look so effortless. But Ronaldo has been playing football daily since he was seven years old. He started his professional career when he was 17, and today he is known as one of the greatest football players of all time. Ronaldo didn't become an expert overnight; he spent 10 years perfecting his craft, and he is still perfecting it although he is considered one of the best football players in the world. This is what consistency does; it turns you into an expert.

I spent many years blaming my parents for my failures in life. This anger intensified the more I learned about how the role of habits plays out in terms of success. I would think to myself, "If my parents had realized I was a good writer when I was a child, they could have gotten me into the habit of writing every day, and I probably would have become a successful author many years ago." While I was correct in my assessment of the role my parents should have played in helping to develop my gift, my parents were only capable of giving me what *their* parents gave *them*. They didn't know anything about success principles. Their main goal was for me to get a good education and find a decent career. As far as they were concerned, they had done their job if I achieved those things. To them, success was following the path society had laid out for me, and it was my job to do what had never been done before in my bloodline—become successful by non-traditional methods. My parents were not in the least bit impressed when I told them my plans of becoming a self-published author. They couldn't understand why I didn't want to climb the corporate ladder and become successful that way. They were more concerned with stability than anything else. I didn't blame my parents for not understanding; like the majority of the world, they had been conditioned by society to think a certain way. The only way I could convince them that my way was the right way was to become successful. And that's exactly what I did—and it was consistency that got me there.

THE BENEFITS OF CONSISTENCY

Not only is consistency the driving force behind success; it also has several other benefits. Here are some of them:

Improves Your Performance: Research suggests that consistency improves performance. A study conducted by the University of Nebraska discovered that people perform better when they work on challenging tasks consistently. This theory has been proven several times. In his book *Atomic Habits*, the *New York Times* bestselling author James Clear relayed the story of the British cycling team. The team had been hanging on to professional cycling by the skin of their teeth for almost 100 years, during which time they had only won one gold medal at the Olympic Games. Their performance was so bad that one of the most successful European bike manufacturers would not sell their bikes to the team because they didn't want to align themselves with their reputation of failure and damage their sales. To help improve the team's performance, they hired performance director Dave Brailsford. He implemented a strategy called "the aggregation of marginal gains," which involved making very small improvements in every area of bike-riding by one percent.

Brailsford's team started by making small adjustments to the bike seats, tires, and the riders' clothes. They worked on making improvements in overlooked areas such as changing massage gels to improve injury recovery times. They learned the most effective way to wash their hands to prevent catching any illnesses that were going around. They changed their pillows and mattresses to get the best night's sleep. The more changes they made, the faster the team's performance improved. Within five years of hiring Brailsford, the British cycling team took over the sport and won several gold medals during the Olympic Games in Beijing. Four years later, the team had set seven world records and nine Olympic records. The team just kept improving, and within 10 years, they had won five Tour de France medals, 66 Olympic gold medals, and 178 world championships.

Establishes Your Reputation: When you learn to consistently show up for yourself, consistency will become a habit, and it will reflect in every area of your life, including your professional and personal lives. I didn't start respecting myself until I developed consistency. It wasn't until I really started analyzing my life that I realized how important consistency was. One of the reasons I was never promoted at work was because of my inconsistency. After being assigned a project, my manager would ask for weekly updates, every Friday before 12:00 p.m. But most of the time, I was late. I eventually developed a reputation for submitting my updates late, and it became a running joke in the office. While my tardiness gave everyone a good laugh, it kept me on a lower paygrade.

The same was true in my relationships. My partners never trusted me because I never did what I said I was going to do. I couldn't understand what the big deal was because as far as I was concerned, it wasn't anything major. I did things like not call when I said I was going to call, cancel dates at the last minute, and turn up late when I *did* show up for a date. To me, these were minor incidents and an apology should have been enough to keep the relationship moving. But what I was doing was showing my partners that I couldn't be trusted because, "How you do anything is how you do everything." (T. Harv Eker.) I was showing them I was unreliable, and their fear was that eventually, I would do something to completely destroy the relationship. When they dumped me, I was the victim and spent hours complaining to my friends about women not knowing what they want in a relationship.

If you want to start a business, you'll need to consistently show your clients that you can deliver, or they will quickly move on to someone else. Isn't it funny how we expect consistency from everyone else—but we are not consistent ourselves? I used to go to this burger joint every Thursday evening for about six months. I went there all the time because the food was delicious; however, for three Thursdays in a row, the food was terrible. The burger was dry, the chips were stale, and the drink was flat. Each time I complained and got a replacement meal, but I got tired of it and moved on to another restaurant. Can you see the pattern here? It was the power of consistency that made me a regular client, and the power of consistency that pushed me into the arms of their competitors. While it's true there is no such thing as the perfect business, and everyone makes mistakes, it is also true that some customers are not going to tolerate a business making the same mistake three times in a row. People are paying for a service, and if they are not getting what they want from one business, they will quickly move on to the next.

Forms Habits: People often give up trying to build good habits because they aim for perfection instead of consistency. The person wanting to go to the gym six days a week will quit if they miss two days because life happens and there will be times when you can't fulfil your commitments. This is known as an "all-or-nothing" mindset, and it can destroy your efforts when you are trying to develop good habits. However, consistency allows you to keep working on your goals even when things happen that are outside of your control. Consistency also prevents feelings of disappointment and frustration when things don't go your way.

Some people procrastinate not because they're lazy but because they're afraid they won't meet the impossibly high standards they've set for themselves. Psychologists refer to procrastination and perfectionism as twins because they are both equally as destructive. Nevertheless, while consistency is the most effective way to develop good habits, people avoid it like the plague because they're looking for a quick fix. The person wanting to lose weight would rather attempt to go on an extreme diet for a few weeks than develop a lifetime habit of healthy eating. But this attitude is counterproductive because you are more likely to quit on an extreme diet, or go back to unhealthy eating once you've lost the weight and quickly put it back on again. Consistently making small behavioral changes won't get you to the finish line faster, but it will ensure that you develop and maintain good habits over the long term.

Builds Mental Toughness: My favorite sport has always been long-distance running. It wasn't until I ran a marathon myself that I fully understood why. Prior to me developing self-discipline, I was fascinated by long-distance runners because I couldn't understand why they would put themselves through such torture. Why would they want to run all those miles? It was ridiculous yet astonishing to me. But when I started reading about the mentality of professional runners, it started to make more sense. Firstly, the training process is about consistency. A marathon runner doesn't start off running 30 miles; they spend about 20 weeks training for it. During this time, their muscles, heart, and mind must be conditioned for the race. A training plan is put together to suit their needs, and it typically looks something like this:

- Go for short runs three days per week.
- Go for longer runs once per week, increasing the length with each run.
- Combine conditioning exercises such as hill sprints with circuit activities.

- Have two to three rest days per week.

- Do non-impact exercises such as yoga, swimming, weights, cycling, and cross-training.

The training helps runners develop the mental toughness required to run the marathon. However, without consistency, it wouldn't be possible to prepare the mind and body to run 30 miles.

How to be Consistent

Consistency is a skill that can be developed if you are willing to practice. Here are some tips on how to do so:

Set Reminders: Unless you have the memory of an elephant, it will be very difficult for you to be consistent because you will forget a lot of things. You can avoid this by creating a schedule for yourself so everything you need to do is written down and planned out. A well-written schedule will give you insight into your commitments and the time you have to fulfill them. You can use a planning app so reminders will go off on your phone, or you can stick Post-it notes around your home.

Don't Overcommit: The worst thing you can do when it comes to consistency is overcommit. Whether it's to yourself or to other people, you will not be able to remain consistent if you try to do too much. In my zeal to be more consistent, I told my ex-girlfriend we would maintain our relationship by going on a date every Friday night. But it didn't take long to realize it was impossible to keep up these weekly date nights because it took time away from my Saturday morning writing routine. I also overcommitted by promising I would give my apartment a deep clean every Sunday. That happened once and never again. It was easier for me to spend half an hour a day cleaning. Basically, don't make promises you can't keep, whether it's to yourself or to others.

Practice Accountability: It's easier to make excuses and place blame on everyone and everything but ourselves when our lives are not going in the direction we desire. For example, you planned on waking up an hour early six days a week to go to the gym, but you hit the snooze button because you keep going to bed late. You keep going to bed late because you're either on the phone talking to your friends, or scrolling. But instead of admitting that your lack of discipline is the reason you keep going to bed late, you make excuses. You blame your friends for phoning you, and you claim that you scroll because you can't sleep. Practicing accountability would mean admitting you are not waking up on time because you go to bed late as a result of the things that you do in the evening. However, once you've admitted this to yourself, you then need to make the necessary changes to ensure you no longer go to bed late. This might mean you tell your friends not to call you after a certain time, and if you find it difficult to sleep at night, look at why. Is it because you drink too much coffee during the day? Are you eating foods in the evening that give you a lot of energy? Research suggests that blue light from screens affects sleep, for example. One way to avoid this is to turn off all screens at least one hour before going to bed. Holding yourself accountable for your actions is a constant reminder that you are the only person responsible for the way your life turns out.

Take a Break: Sundays are my day of rest; I do nothing but relax and recharge. If I choose to socialize, I won't make it too heavy, but keep the day short and sweet. Taking a break at least once a week protects you from burnout so you don't end up needing to take an extended break.

Don't Give Up: Consistency is a skill you develop over time with practice. However, it is not an easy skill to develop, and it will take a lot of time and dedication. You are not going to get it right immediately; some days you will be consistent, and others you won't. But as long as you never give up, you will eventually develop the habit of consistency.

When I started learning about success principles, I got so excited that I told all my friends about it. Unfortunately, they were nowhere near as enthusiastic as I was, and when I began applying the principles I was learning, our relationships crumbled. One of the reasons some people don't achieve their goals is because they don't want to lose their friends. If your friends are not willing to join you on this journey, you'll need to make a choice between your friends and living your dream life. In Chapter 11, you'll find out why.

CHAPTER 11:

FRIENDS NO MORE: YOU CAN'T TAKE EVERYONE TO THE TOP

"Make friends who force you to level up."
—Unknown

Unfortunately, when you decide to start working on your goals, it's highly likely that your friends won't be ready to start working on theirs (if they have any). Indeed, according to research, only 3% of the population set goals. Your friends have put you in a box; they know you for being XYZ, and they expect you to be that way for the rest of your life. They can't imagine you changing, and they don't want you to change—because if you change, you won't have anything in common with them anymore. So, they'll do everything in their power to attempt to sabotage your efforts, and if you're not strong enough, you'll let them. Despite the fact that they've spent years complaining to you about how much they hate their life, the moment you start making changes, all of a sudden they're more than happy with what they've got. The truth is that the majority of people are not satisfied with life, and if they could click their fingers and get what they want, they would. But most people either don't know how to get what they want, or they don't have the self-discipline required to do so. Instead, they waste time dreaming about the life they want and complaining about why they can't have it. Sadly, you'll either end up ditching most of your friends, or they'll ditch you. It will hurt, and you won't want to, but you've got to make a choice: you can either stay at the bottom of the mountain with them, or climb to greater heights. Take your pick!

How Your Friends Will Distract You

For most of you reading this, the friends you have right now are going to be a major source of distraction when you start working on your goals. And this is typically how the distractions will manifest:

Constant Phone Calls: In some form or another, I spent several hours a night on the phone to my friends. Whether we were texting, talking, or sending each other clips from social media, we were constantly glued to our phones, and if I didn't respond instantly, there would be a barrage of texts or calls until I did. If one of them posted something on social media and I didn't like the post immediately, I would get a text or a phone call asking if I'd seen the post. There was no way I could get anything done with this amount of distraction. When I say my phone was constantly pinging, I mean it was literally nonstop—and I was there staring at my phone with my thumbs ready.

Inviting You to Go Out: When you have no purpose or direction in life, you are always ready for anything. Anytime a friend called to go out, I was down. It didn't matter whether it was during the week and I'd end up getting home late and having just a couple of hours' sleep—as long as I didn't miss out on the fun, I was more than happy to tag along. Once you decide to start working on your goals, you will realize how important time is, and you won't be able to go out as much. But because your friends don't understand that extreme sacrifice is a part of the journey to success, they'll keep inviting you out and will get very offended when you turn the offers down. Initially, you will feel guilty—for me, it took a while before I could say no without feeling bad. But I knew that if I kept going out, I would never get anything done, and I had to make a choice. It was either my friends or my goals. I chose my goals.

Can't Stick to One Thing: On our quest to become wealthy, we were always searching for the next get-rich-quick scheme. One week it was real estate; the next it was drop-shipping; then trading—the list was endless. We would watch a couple of YouTube videos, have a meeting, draw up a plan about what we were going to do to cash in on this new idea, get excited, high-five each other, buy a few books, never read them, and then give up when we realized how much work was actually involved. A few weeks later, we would jump on the next bandwagon. But we were wasting our time for two main reasons. I'm sure these get-rich-quick schemes were profitable, but none of us were actually prepared to do the work necessary to reap the benefits. Also, we didn't really understand what we were doing. We were all very talented and creative individuals. My friend Jake was an excellent carpenter; everything in his house he built himself. He could have built a very successful carpentry business, but he didn't want to do the work. My other friend Clive was a fantastic barber; he cut all our hair—he was so good that we refused to go to anyone else. He could have built a very successful barber's business, but he didn't want to do the work. My other friend was a very gifted mechanic; he could tell what was wrong with a car just by listening to the engine. He could have built a very successful mechanic's business, but he didn't want to do the work.

All of my friends had a gift they could have profited from, but they were too busy chasing fast money to invest in the thing they were actually good at. My gift was writing, and I used it to become successful. I knew nothing about real estate, investing, or any of the other industries that are so heavily promoted as ways to become wealthy. However, I trusted that if I invested in my gift, I would eventually reap the benefits—and that's exactly what I did. This was another reason my friends laughed at me. They were adamant that unless I got as lucky as Stephen King, becoming an author would never make me rich. Well, I proved them wrong!

I truly believe that we were all born with a gift that can make us rich. It doesn't matter what it is. One such example is an ordinary lady from New York called Janie Deegan. She is the founder of Janie's Life-Changing Baked Goods, a bakery worth over a million dollars. She developed a love for baking because it helped calm her anxiety and kept her sober. Janie is a former alcoholic, but after getting clean and realizing she had a baking talent, she started selling her baked goods and got an overwhelming response. She was making money doing the thing she loved the most. After several years of hustling, she opened a bricks-and-mortar store, and then a second, and a third. Today, she is a multimillionaire. Basically, your gift will open doors for you. Once you've perfected your craft, people will pay you big money for it. But the problem is that people don't want to spend time perfecting their craft.

I believe that there are plenty of people in the world more talented than the late Michael Jackson and the late Kobe Bryant. The problem is they are too lazy to do the work required to polish their talent in order to gain the attention of the people they need to help make them successful. Unless you are born into a rich family, you will never become wealthy overnight. Michael Jackson started singing at the age of five but didn't make his recording debut until the age of nine. He practiced for four years before getting any type of recognition for his talent. Kobe Bryant started playing basketball at the age of three, and he didn't get drafted until he was 17. That's 14 years' worth of practice. The reality of the situation is that the universe isn't going to just *give* you what you want—it is going to *test* you to determine whether you actually want it or not. How many hours of practice are you willing to put in? How many failures are you willing to endure? How many sacrifices are you willing to make? My first three books were total flops; none of them sold any more than 100 copies. But those few sales gave me hope. It was evidence that there were people interested in buying my books—I just had to find them, and that's what I focused my energy on. Had I given up after the first three books, I wouldn't be where I am today.

Negative Energy: I'm actually a fan of constructive criticism because if you don't know where you're going wrong, how can you improve? However, what I'm *not* a fan of is people who infect the atmosphere with negativity. Let me explain. When I started writing, a friend wanted to come and visit because he was concerned about my lack of contact. Stupidly, I agreed.

My apartment was spotless, and not because I had cleaned up because my friend was coming over, but because I had developed a habit of keeping it clean. The first thing he said when he walked in was, "Do you actually live here? Your apartment looks like a show home! There's absolutely no need for it to be this neat." One might take that as a compliment, but I sensed that the statement was laced with underlying jealousy. He knew my energy had completely shifted because he was used to walking into a state of chaos. Previously, I had lived like a slob, and so did all my friends; it was the norm for us to trip over pizza boxes when we walked into each other's houses. The first thing I told him to do was put some booties over his shoes because I don't do dirty feet walking all over my clean floors. Jason looked at me like I had lost my mind and screeched, "Are you serious?" before reluctantly putting them on. When he got into my living room, I could see him looking around as if he was in a foreign environment. He then proceeded to sit on the edge of the sofa and mumbled, "I wouldn't want to ruin your million-dollar sofa with my crusty clothes."

When he realized I had no TV, he asked, "Are you okay? Is there something you need to tell me? Why would you need to sell your TV?" I explained that my television was a distraction and so I'd gotten rid of it. "A distraction? This is not normal behavior. Normal people have TVs." I gave him an hour, and during that time, he had nothing good to say. He just sat there telling me how much I was missing out on, and that no amount of success was worth losing all your friends over. And did I really think I could become a millionaire writing books? He whipped out his phone and did the calculations, stating that over 100,000 people would need to buy my book to make a million dollars. He reminded me that I didn't even have 500 social media followers, so how on earth was I going to achieve these goals I had set for myself? He told me I was setting myself up for failure, and that I should be more realistic or I would end up depressed because I'd set unrealistic goals and had lost all my friends trying to achieve them.

When he first started speaking, I was tempted to throw him out. But I listened because I wanted to confirm that I had made the right choice in ditching my friends. Deep down, I knew I had, but I needed to be sure. If that's what Jason thought, that's what the rest of my friends thought because I knew, without a shadow of a doubt, that they spent a lot of time talking about me. Because it was clear that I had distanced myself from everyone, Jason had been sent as the spy to find out what was going on. His job was to snoop and report back to the crew. I didn't need negative energy around me, so ending those friendships wasn't a loss. May I add that they hadn't suddenly developed this negative energy—that's just how they were. When I was hanging around them, that's how I was too. I remember us talking about one guy we went to high school with who dropped out to start his own computer company. He became very wealthy, and everyone knew about him. He was richer than all of us, he didn't have a college degree, and his parents weren't rich. We would have extended conversations about what we thought he'd done to become successful, and we didn't have anything good to say. We came up with all types of conspiracy theories that he had sold his soul to the devil, that he had joined the Masonic lodge, or maybe he had slept his way to the top. It was ridiculous. Because *we* were too lazy to do the work to become successful, we assumed everyone else was too.

We live in a negative world, so positive people are seen as an anomaly. When you turn on the TV, open a newspaper, magazine, or listen to the radio, all you hear is bad news. It's very easy to be negative because it's the norm. Just stand in any area populated by people having conversations, and nine times out of ten, they won't have anything good to say. At work all you hear is negativity. When you go home all you hear is negativity. Log on to social media and all you hear is negativity. Meet up with your friends or speak to them on the phone and all you hear is negativity. You are literally surrounded by it, and it takes an exceptional amount of self-discipline to remain positive when everything you hear is negative. Negativity is like a poison that infects your thoughts. If all your friends talk about is how impossible it is to become successful unless you know the right people, guess what? You will convince yourself that it's a complete waste of time attempting to achieve your goals because you don't know the right people. As in my situation, when you break out of that mindset and start working on your goals, your friends will do everything they can to block your progress with their negativity. I almost fell into their trap several times, and it took a lot of mental restraint not to absorb their negative energy. This was especially true when my books didn't sell. I hadn't blocked or unfollowed any of my friends on social media, and nor had they blocked or unfollowed me. A couple of months after releasing my first book, I only had one Amazon review and it was clear that the book hadn't done well. I got a message from one of my ex-friends saying, "Congratulations, big-time author. How does it feel to have ditched your friends only to fail?" As upsetting as it was, I didn't let that message discourage me from writing more books.

Shortly after I became a bestseller, I met a very successful clothes designer called Adrian at a networking event. He is one of my closest friends now and makes all of my clothes. When he first started his clothing line, he invested thousands into the business, but he didn't sell anything. He had boxes of clothes in his parents' house collecting dust. His mom and dad meant well by indirectly advising him to give up on his dreams, get a regular job and settle down. But he closed his ears to the naysayers and persevered. Today, his clothing line is worth millions, and many celebrities support his brand by not only wearing his clothes but also purchasing bespoke pieces designed by him. Had he given up, he would never have achieved such massive success. Adrian kept his eyes focused on a vision only he could see, and eventually, he reaped what he had sown. I implore you, don't ever give up on your dreams. The journey is excruciating, and you are going to have to claw your way to the top. Nothing of great value will manifest in your life if you don't have the drive and the determination to persevere in the face of adversity. Push through the pain because on the other side awaits the life you've been dreaming about. This is a fight only you can win. Don't throw in the towel.

Why It Matters Who You Are Friends With

When I was a teenager, my parents hated most of my friends because they thought they were a bad influence on me—which they were. They would always say to me, "Show me your friend, and I'll show you your character." Basically, you are who you hang around with; like attracts like. When I began taking inventory of my friends, I realized this was true—I was exactly like my friends. We all had no ambition, no drive, and we refused to take responsibility for our lives. We all played the blame game and pointed the finger at our families for not being rich enough to set us up for life. We all wanted an easy way out, which was why we played the lottery every week. We had made a promise to each other that if any of us won the jackpot, we would split the money equally between ourselves. But of course, none of us ever won the lottery, and nor were we willing to do the work required to earn the millions we so desired. But when I started reading about success principles and decided to take my life seriously, none of my friends wanted to do the same. They thought I was living in dreamland and that I would never achieve what I had set out to achieve. Their negative comments were all I heard, and for a while, they made me doubt myself. I began to wonder whether there was any point in me even trying. But then I read a quote by motivational speaker Jim Rohn that said, "You are the average of the five people you spend the most time with." After reading this, the penny dropped instantly; I realized that if I didn't stop hanging around with my friends, I would never change. I needed to surround myself with people who wanted to get somewhere in life and were willing to do the work required.

It took a while to let go of them completely, for several reasons, but one of them was because I thought I wouldn't have anyone to share my success with when I made it. I thought I would be missing out on something. What was life going to be like at the top with no friends? What would be the point of achieving my goals and having no one to celebrate with? But it didn't take long for me to realize that, even if I did keep them as friends, there wouldn't be a real celebration anyway because they would never be truly happy for me. The insults and the lack of respect I received for choosing my dreams instead of them let me know that these were not the people I needed in my life anyway.

Loneliness Is a Part of the Journey

Becoming successful is about working on a dream that only you can see. You hold a picture in your mind, and you are doing what needs to be done to turn it into reality. When I first told my friends I couldn't go out on the weekends like I used to because I was writing a book, they laughed. They laughed because they didn't believe I was capable of pulling off something so grand, considering I was known for never finishing anything. I didn't blame them for laughing; they didn't trust me because I had shown them with my actions that I couldn't be trusted to do anything I said I was going to do. Every year it was the same story—I was going to lose weight and get shredded like the men we looked at in magazines. It never happened. But we were all the same, so it was a running joke amongst us that we were a bunch of losers who were never going to achieve anything in life. However, this time was different, and I could feel it. We'd had the same routine for years; every Friday, we would bar-hop and get totally drunk. Saturday was spent in bed nursing a hangover, then we'd go out for dinner in the evening and hit a couple more bars. We spent Sundays in bed, complaining on the phone about how we didn't want to go to work on Monday. Unless one of us had something else to do, that was the routine. But after two months of me continuously rejecting their offers to go out, they started getting nasty. They would send me rude text messages saying things like, "You're taking writing a book way too seriously. You can't just come out for one drink?" Or, "Do you think you're better than us now you've decided to become an amateur author?" I got seriously offended by these messages and wasted a lot of time arguing back and forth with them, trying to get them to understand where I was coming from. But mentally, they were not on my level—and I'm not saying that to be boastful. I had transcended to another mental dimension, and as far as they were concerned, there was something wrong with me.

You see, it's not the norm to stay at home on the weekends working on your goals. Society has conditioned us to believe that the weekends are for partying, and if you're not partying then you're boring, and there's something wrong with you. My work colleagues even started asking me if I was okay. On Monday mornings, I usually had loads of stories to tell about my escapades over the weekend, but not anymore. My weekends were spent writing, so when they asked, I just said it was quiet. I didn't see the point in trying to convince another group of people that I was writing a book.

For two years straight, I did nothing but stay at home and write. I became a complete hermit. I lost all my friends, and my family thought I'd turned into a mad scientist—but I didn't care; I knew what I needed to do to succeed. Was it lonely? Absolutely! But if I didn't make some big sacrifices, my life wasn't going to change. I was tired of living below my potential. Although I wasn't successful yet, I had developed the mentality of a successful person and I was finding it increasingly difficult to be around "normal" people. My standards had become higher than average, and I was thinking about things that the people I was around couldn't identify with. I started to have less and less in common with my family members and my work colleagues. I was operating in a spirit of excellence; becoming great was non-negotiable for me—there was no plan B. To ensure I became my highest self, I had to avoid mediocrity and everyone connected to it. Not everyone values excellence; people are always trying to cut corners. Again, this meant I had less in common with others.

When I was unsuccessful, I couldn't relate to the way successful people lived. I prejudged them as being full of themselves. Maybe some of them are, but I know now, from interacting with a lot of successful people, that the majority are far from full of themselves. They make massive sacrifices, they have a tremendous amount of ambition and drive, and they want to be the best in their field. All of which means they have no time to socialize or do much other than work to accomplish their goals. They are committed to living up to their potential, and this is a foreign concept to most people. I found it extremely draining to have to keep explaining myself to people. There was no point because they just didn't understand. I found it easier to withdraw. I stopped caring that they thought I was crazy.

I wanted to grow and become better every day; it was a high priority of mine. I began to live an intentional lifestyle of self-improvement, and I had an unquenchable appetite to digest the wisdom and knowledge required to become the person I was destined to be. I set strict boundaries and refused to allow anything into my life that would hinder my progress. Again, people didn't like this, but I didn't care; I wasn't going to allow anything or anyone to stop me.

I became very clear about my values and worth, and anyone around me or trying to get close to me who didn't have similar values was quickly eliminated from my life. One of the things I stopped tolerating was drama. For many years, I was the biggest drama queen. There was always something negative going on in my life or in a friend's life, and I would force myself right in the middle of it. But when I developed self-worth, I realized how unhealthy drama was. It kept me in a negative state of mind, and it left me with very little time to do anything productive. Once I changed my mindset, people who didn't have any self-worth or values became very draining. They were like leeches; they added nothing to my life—all they did was take.

I felt very lonely during this time. But I didn't allow it to get me down. I read a lot of self-help books and autobiographies by successful people, and I discovered that loneliness is a part of the journey. It is a necessary part of the process. Not only do you get the time to do the things you need to do to succeed, you also learn more about yourself. Eventually, you'll start meeting like-minded people, and you can start going out again and having a social life, but it will never be the same as before. Successful people don't have the time to paint the town red every weekend. Now I make sure I do something fun once a month, and I have sensible, like-minded friends to go out with.

One of the things your old friends will attempt to do is break down your will and get you to come out at least once. It will be very tempting because of the loneliness, and your mind will start playing tricks on you, trying to convince you that one last time won't hurt. Well, it *will* hurt. I know because I gave in to my friends' begging and pleading. Don't fold. Because the moment you do, two things will happen: they will lose respect for you; and you'll break your momentum, and it will be hard to get back into flow mode. That night was the worst night out I've ever had. I was miserable the entire time. I was the butt of all jokes, with my friends spending the evening poking fun at me for not having had enough willpower to say no. After that, it took me almost a month to get back into the swing of things.

One of the things that really helped me stay focused was healthy eating, and every Sunday, I meal-prepped. But that Sunday, I was too hungover to meal-prep. I had eaten a takeout the night before, and now I felt justified in having another one. I told myself I had already given into the temptation of junk food, so I might as well continue. So, I ordered more takeout, and some snacks and soda to get me through the night. Then I told myself that, since I was hungover, there was no point in me trying to write so I might as well see what was going down on social media. Then I migrated to YouTube and spent the rest of the night watching nonsense.

But this binge didn't end there. I woke up late on Monday morning because I stayed up until around 2:00 a.m. watching YouTube videos, which meant I had no time for breakfast or lunch, so I grabbed something on my way to work. When I got home, the house was a mess, and I was exhausted from having had a late night and eating junk food all day, so I couldn't be bothered to cook and ordered more takeout. Can you see the downward spiral of decline, and how quickly this turned into a disaster? One night ruined everything. Don't make the same mistake. It's not worth it.

Stop Caring About What Other People Think

It's human nature to want the approval of our peers. However, when it comes to the success game, you'll need pretty thick skin. Success is not for the faint-hearted, and if you can't handle criticism, you might as well throw in the towel now. The majority of your friends, family members, and loved ones are not going to respect your hustle until they see results. Even then, some of them still won't respect you; they'll start hating on you instead. It will hurt that the people you care about the most won't celebrate with you, but that's just the way it is, and you'll need to get used to it. Unfortunately, your enemies are not the ones watching from afar—they're in your house, they're breaking bread with you, they are the people closest to you. When it comes to money, your family members will stab you in the back quicker than anyone else. Look at how many siblings of celebrities have sold them out to the press. Madonna's brother Christopher Ciccone; Brittney Spears' sister, Jamie Lynn; Mariah Carey's sister, Alison Carey—the list is endless. People will try and discredit you; they'll laugh at you, they'll call you a failure. But you can't afford to allow the opinions of others to discourage you from fulfilling your purpose. It's definitely easier said than done, but the stronger your mind gets, the easier it will become. Here are some signs that you are too consumed with others' opinions of you:

- You change your behavior when you are criticized, regardless of who said it and why.
- You allow other people to make your decisions.
- You either have no boundaries, or you allow people to violate them.
- You're a perfectionist.
- You won't state your opinion if it is not the same as everyone else's.
- You only have peace of mind when you get approval from others.
- You say yes to everything.
- You apologize even when it's not your fault.

Here are some tips on how to stop caring so much about what other people think about you:

Expect It: It's amazing how we have opinions about people but we don't like it when other people have opinions about us. Let that sink in for a minute! The reality is that everyone has opinions about everyone; some of them are good, some of them are bad, and there really isn't much we can do about it. The most talented and wealthy people in the world have critics. What makes you any different?

Control Your Emotions: While you can't control how people feel about you, you *can* control how *you* feel about their opinions. The minute you hear something you don't like, you have the choice to react to it or let it slide. This isn't about burying your emotions; it's about acknowledging how you feel, managing those feelings and releasing them. Whatever you need to do to release your emotions, do that and keep it moving. Don't allow your emotions to control you by holding a grudge.

Build Your Confidence: Confident people don't have time to care about what others think about them, because they know who they are. When you're unsure of yourself, you'll allow other people's opinions to define you because you're constantly seeking validation. By developing your confidence, you free yourself from trying to be 25 different people at once, and you can rest comfortably in the knowledge of who you are. When you're concerned about how you're perceived, you often try to conform to what other people want you to be. When their opinion changes, you change—and your life will continue like this until you get tired of wearing a mask and go on a journey of self-discovery.

Consider the Source: When I started writing my book, my friends and family members were my main critics. However, they had yet to achieve anything significant in life. You will find that your biggest haters are people who don't have anything better to do with their time. They have no goals, no ambitions, and no purpose, so they're constantly poking their noses into other people's business looking for something to criticize them about. These are the individuals who know all about the latest celebrity gossip, but they're the same ones who will say they don't have time to start a side hustle! Basically, if you're not getting constructive criticism from someone who has achieved a level of success that you admire, don't let it bother you. Why should you care about the opinion of someone whose main hobby is criticizing people?

PREPARE TO BE LABELED AS CRAZY

As I've said throughout this book, we live in a world where we've been conditioned to believe there is only one road to a happy life. And that is to go to school, get an education, find a decent career to work in for forty years, get married, have a few kids, retire in your old age and then explore the world after you've given your everything to the system, so much so that you have no energy left to do anything but sit in a rocking chair in a retirement home waiting to die. Sounds pessimistic, but that's the reality of the majority of people's lives. They are too scared to follow their dreams because it's not the norm. To really keep people in their place, society ostracizes those who break out of the constraints of conformity and dare to follow their hearts, and labels them as crazy. Friends and family laugh at them and mock them for following a dream only they can see. No one believes in them—until that dream becomes a reality, and everyone else can see what they've been incubating in their heads for so long.

The good news is that if you've been labeled as crazy, you're on the right path because a lot of successful people were labeled as crazy! It looks like it's a part of the process. Here are some of them:

Arnold Schwarzenegger: Most famously known for his role as "the Terminator," the Austrian actor laughs about it in interviews today, but in his younger years, when he told his parents he wanted to be a body-building champion, they told him it was an impossible dream because only Americans became body builders. When he covered his wall in pictures of body builders, his parents thought he had lost his mind and that he might be gay because his bedroom wall was covered in pictures of half-naked men. In an attempt to "cure" him, they sent him to a psychiatrist.

Albert Einstein: Today, Albert Einstein is a well-respected physicist, primarily known for his theory of relativity. However, when he was alive, his unorthodox theories challenged traditional views of physics, and his peers found them extremely difficult to understand. Additionally, he didn't conform to the norms and standards of his day in terms of his image. His hair was all over the place and his clothes were disheveled. Einstein was completely obsessed with his work; he probably read more books and studied more than the average physician and was therefore a lot more intelligent than his counterparts, hence they thought he was crazy.

Ignaz Semmelweis: Ignaz Semmelweis was ridiculed in the mid-19th century because he called for doctors to wash their hands to prevent the spread of infectious diseases on maternity wards. He argued that medical staff should wash their hands with a solution of chlorinated lime before tending to patients. This practice was unheard of because the medical community had a limited understanding of germ theory. As a result, he faced many professional challenges, and his theory did not gain traction until his death. Today, handwashing to prevent the spread of germs is considered of the utmost importance, not only in hospitals but in everyday life.

Galileo Galilei: Galileo Galilei was an Italian astronomer, engineer, physicist, and polymath who played a critical role in the scientific revolution of the 17th century. He discovered that the earth travels around the sun. The Catholic church considered his findings heretical because they contradicted what was written in the Bible—that the sun traveled around the earth. They were so against his theory that they labeled him a madman and put him on trial. Galilei was found guilty, forced to renounce his theory and placed on house arrest for the rest of his life. Science later found his ideas to be true.

All of these men thought outside of the box and refused to be restrained by society's standards. Some of them didn't gain the recognition they deserved until they had been dead for several years. If you are going to be successful, you'll need to have a little crazy in you. Here's why:

Crazy People Don't Care What Other People Think: If I cared what my friends and family thought about me, I would have stopped writing after the failure of my first book. For years, I locked myself in my house, cut off my friends and had limited contact with family because I desperately believed in my dream to become an author. After my first book failed, the tongues started wagging. After the second book failed, the tongues continued to wag. After the third book failed, I think they must have believed I was a complete lunatic because they stopped sending me pity messages. But I didn't care—I knew what I wanted, and I was going to get it by any means necessary. And that's exactly what I did. Now I'm known as the person who was crazy enough to keep chasing a dream that appeared to be running away from me.

Crazy People Think Outside the Box: It's not normal to prioritize your dreams instead of climbing the corporate ladder. Most people are obsessed with running someone else's company instead of becoming their own boss. The minute you start talking about starting your own business, you'll get plenty of side-eyes, especially if it's doing something they can't see working. My friends and family would have been more accepting of my goals if I'd planned on getting a publishing deal. But self-publishing was unheard of, and people didn't think it was possible to become a successful author selling your own books. However, I knew it was possible because it was working for a lot of self-published authors. While it wasn't working for all of them, and many people were complaining about how unprofitable it was, I chose to follow the blueprint of the authors who were successful—and eventually, I made it too.

Crazy People Don't Follow the Rules: To become an author, the rule is to write a book, send it to dozens of publishing companies and wait for one of them to accept you. If a publishing company does decide to publish your book, they'll pay you an advance, and then a percentage of each book sale for the duration of the time the book is available. Self-published authors have developed a terrible reputation for being the bad writers that the publishing houses rejected. Despite this stigma, I chose to self-publish anyway. I always knew I wanted to self-publish rather than go down the traditional route. I refused to follow the rules, and it paid off.

Crazy People Don't Accept No: Since my first, second, and third books failed, it appeared as if the universe wasn't pleased with me and was giving me a sign that this dream of mine wasn't such a good idea after all. But I refused to take no for an answer. I knew deep within my soul that I was doing the right thing. I just didn't know when it was going to work out for me. I hated my job, and I desperately wanted to leave, but writing books wasn't paying me enough to buy a sandwich for lunch each day, let alone pay my bills, so I had to keep working. Those three nos didn't stop me from continuing to pursue my dreams. Failure didn't scare me; I lived by Thomas Edison's principle: "I have not failed. I've just found 10,000 ways that won't work." I had made up my mind that I was going to keep going until I found what worked for me.

Crazy People Believe in Themselves: It's very easy to believe in yourself when everything is going your way. But what do you do when it's not? The dictionary definition of "believe" is: "To accept that something is true, especially without proof." I had no evidence that I was going to succeed. In fact, the only evidence I was staring at was that of failure. But I refused to accept the evidence of failure and focused on the strength I knew I had within me to persevere, despite three failed attempts at publishing my books. I had the audacity to believe in myself even though no one was interested in buying my books. It would have made more sense for me to say, "Rest in peace" to my dreams than continue, when becoming a self-published author clearly wasn't working for me. A psychiatrist would have said I was delusional. The dictionary definition of the word "delusional" is: "Characterized by or holding false beliefs or judgments about external reality that are held despite incontrovertible evidence to the contrary, typically as a symptom of a mental condition." And then in brackets it says, "Hospitalization for schizophrenia and delusional paranoia."

By definition, all successful people are crazy, because their idea started in their mind. The seed was a thought; they created a plan and worked on it until it became a reality. The person striving for success works on something they can't see with their physical eyes until they *can* see it. The best definition of faith I've heard is, "Faith is the substance of things hoped for, and the evidence of things not seen." Isn't that interesting? You are hoping for something that you have no evidence of because you haven't seen it. The mind has been conditioned to only believe in what the eyes can see. It literally takes a crazy person to go against the grain and choose to believe in something they can't see.

Crazy People Don't Need Approval: When I decided to write my first book, I didn't go around asking my friends and family members what they thought of my idea because I had no desire for their approval. I knew they wouldn't understand what I was trying to do until it was done. I told people what I was doing when I started doing it, and as I suspected, I got no support whatsoever. If I was the type of person who needed everyone to agree with me before I did anything, I would never have started. As I've mentioned, you are the only person who can see your dream. The people you tell can't see it, so what's the point of asking for their permission to start working on it? Don't wait for the green light from anyone—just put your foot on the accelerator and go!

Crazy People Are Motivated by Passion: Passionate people are rare because they know their purpose and what they were put on this earth to do. They have a clear vision for their life, and they're actively working to actualize it. Passionate people don't sit around all day talking about their passions. They are passionate because they know they have a higher calling than the lie society has fed them. They know they're not the same as everyone else because when they're in rooms with average people having average conversations about celebrity gossip and other nonsensical subjects, it disturbs their spirit. Passionate people have specific personality traits. Here are some of them:

- **Energetic:** I'm assuming you are a passionate person, or you wouldn't be reading this book. Being energetic doesn't mean you're an extrovert and bouncing all over the place—indeed, I'm the biggest introvert. But it *does* mean you have a certain level of enthusiasm about your work. When someone asks you questions about it, it's clear you're passionate about it because you speak about it with strong enthusiasm. Passionate people are also adamant about protecting their energy. They don't waste their time trying to explain their passion to those with negative energy. As soon as they sense that what they're saying isn't being well received, they put an abrupt end to the conversation and get away from that person.

- **Authentic:** While everything on the face of the earth has already been done thousands of times over, and there is nothing new under the sun, when *you* do it, it will be original. Thousands of authors write self-help books—so what makes *me* authentic? I have my own stories to tell. All self-help books contain the same principles; they are not saying anything that hasn't already been said. However, what is new is how *my* life experiences reflect the truth of these principles. I'm not trying to copy Tony Robbins, Mark Manson, or Brené Brown, because I have my *own* journey to talk about. I'm not simply parroting information because I know it sells. My story belongs to me, and I'm not trying to appeal to everyone. There are a select group of people who will resonate with my story, and they are the people I want to reach. When I first started my journey, I read about the story of E. L. James, the author of *50 Shades of Grey*. Her self-published book has sold over 100 million copies worldwide! The press ripped her writing ability to shreds, saying that the book was poorly written, but that didn't stop people from buying it. Her story motivated me to pursue my self-publishing career, and my hope is that my story will inspire others to pursue their self-publishing careers—or any other goals they hope to achieve. My authentic story has changed lives, and so can yours.

- **Self-Motivated:** Until I left home to go to college, I never once set an alarm clock because my mom woke me up Monday through Friday. I didn't need to be self-motivated during this time because I had help. But once I started working on my goals, I was on my own. No one was coming to help me achieve them. On the days when I didn't feel like it, I had to get up and get on with it if I was serious about succeeding. No amount of thinking about, dreaming about, or talking about your goals is going to make them manifest. Action is your only option, and if you're not motivated to take action every day, you might as well kiss your dreams goodbye because without hard work, they will never come to fruition.

- **Resilient:** It takes grit and determination to keep working on something that seems to be a total failure. Passionate people are resilient because they are willing to suffer hardship for the thing they care about the most. Giving up on your passion is like suicide because you're literally killing a part of yourself. Resilient people have the ability to cope with the obstacles, stresses, and challenges that come with pursuing your purpose. They know that obstacles are a part of the journey because every passionate person in pursuit of success goes through the same thing. Obstacles are a part of the blueprint for success, and if you can't handle them, this game isn't for you.

- **Open-Minded:** Passionate people are open-minded because they're always on the lookout for something else to be passionate about. They are open to changing the strategies required to achieve their goals. They are flexible, and know they may need to make some adjustments if they are going to succeed, and they are okay with that. Think about it like this: you're on your way to a friend's birthday party and you decide to take the route you normally take to get to their house, but on the way, you get stuck in a traffic jam. You sit in the traffic jam for about 30 minutes before noticing a slip road that has just become visible on your left. Do you take the risk of waiting in the traffic jam not knowing how long it will take before it starts moving, or do you take the slip road and find another way to your friend's house? Most people will take the slip road despite being unfamiliar with the route. The end goal is the same—you've just taken a different route.

I took a self-publishing course and used the strategies I had learned to publish my first three books, but it clearly wasn't working. So I paid more money (money that I didn't have) to take another self-publishing course, and it was completely different to the first one. The result? I became a bestseller and sold thousands of copies! I didn't change the goal—I changed the strategy.

My message to you is: shoot for crazy—you don't want to be normal, EVER! Normal means working a 9–5 and being "safe." Normal means thinking about your dreams, talking about your dreams, but never having the guts to turn them into reality. That's what the majority of people do—and you don't want to be a part of the majority.

How to Ditch Your Friends

It's human nature to feel bad about ditching your friends. I went to high school with mine; we'd been friends for over a decade. But the reality is that not everyone is meant to be in your life forever. When you realize that they are either not ready to change, or they are never going to change, and that it's not your job to change them, it will become much easier to let go of your friends. Most of your friends will just fall off, and you won't need to have this conversation with them, but some of them won't get the message and will hang on for dear life. I only had one friend like this, and eventually, I just had to let him know that I was ending the friendship. When I realized I had to distance myself from my friends, I didn't want to burn any bridges and tell them outright, so I withdrew, hoping they would catch on. I started out by putting everyone on "Do Not Disturb," which meant they could no longer call me when they wanted to. It gave me control over when I spoke to them because when I saw the missed call, it was up to me whether I called back—and most of the time I didn't. Since they couldn't reach me by phone, they started bombarding me with text messages. I had turned off all notifications so I only saw their messages when I went into the messages section. Most of the time I ignored them, or if I did respond, I wasn't having long drawn-out conversations the way I used to. As mentioned, most of them quickly got the hint that I didn't want to be bothered with them anymore. But there was this one friend, Gareth, who just didn't get the message. He kept calling even though he could never get through and I didn't call him back, and he kept messaging even though I rarely responded. One day, I bumped into him at the store, and he was like, "Oh, my goodness, I've been trying so hard to get in touch with you. What's up?" I mustered up the courage right there and then to let him know I had outgrown the friendship. Of course he wasn't very happy about it, but I didn't hear from him again.

 What I discovered was that ending a platonic relationship is similar to ending a romantic relationship. Initially, I took the route of phasing out the friendships, but when I thought about it, I decided that wasn't fair. I took that route because I found it extremely exhausting having to explain to everyone why I wasn't as available and as engaged as I used to be. It was a waste of time because they didn't understand how important it was to make extreme sacrifices for success. However, when I put myself in their shoes, I realized I would be hurt, confused, and worried if all of a sudden my friend's behavior towards me changed and they stopped responding to messages, I couldn't get through to them on the phone, and they kept rejecting invites out. I would assume I had done something to offend my friend, and they were so angry they couldn't bring themselves to tell me. Or they were going through some type of depression. I would have sleepless nights about it. In terms of a romantic relationship, phasing it out is a coward's way to end it. Basically, the best way to end any type of relationship is to have an honest conversation about it. Here are some tips:

Plan: Just like a romantic break-up, it's best to end the relationship face to face instead of over the phone or via text message. Call each one of your friends and tell them you need to talk, and ask when is the best time and place to meet up. Once you've organized the meet-up, you need to prepare yourself for what you are going to say.

Practice: What you don't want to do is bottle it when you're sitting face to face and pretend as if you wanted to talk about something else. To boost your confidence, prepare for what you're going to say because conversations of this nature are difficult. Get yourself a notepad and pen, take a seat, and think about what you are going to talk about. Write down all the reasons why you feel you need to end the friendship. Remember, as much as you don't want to hurt anyone's feelings, honesty is the best policy, and this is about you and not them. There's no need to be rude—don't say things like, "You're not on my level anymore," or, "I don't have the patience or the energy to carry you on my back as I scale the mountain of success." Instead, use the negative sandwich technique, where you start by telling them how great they are, then you deliver the bad news, and finally close with something positive. For example, you might say something like:

"You are such an amazing person. You've helped me through so much since we've been friends. We've had such an awesome time together, and I will be forever grateful for our friendship. However, I'm on a different journey at the moment and I can't keep up with the partying, constant conversations, texting, and social media engagement. I need to focus on my goals, and that means cutting a lot of things out of my life for the time being, including certain friendships, and unfortunately, you're one of them. You haven't done anything wrong; I'm not angry with you, I'm not upset with you, but I just need to devote all my energy towards my goals. What I need from you is for you to stop contacting me altogether. Again, it's not that you've done anything wrong; it's just that I'm going to have tunnel vision for a while, and I'm not sure how long that's going to be. I want the best for you, I really do. I'll call you and let you know all about it when I'm done."

You've been very clear and direct in this conversation without being rude. You haven't caused offense because you've shouldered the blame. You've also left the ball in your court by saying you'll call them when you're done, which means it's up to you whether you call them again or not. It's a complete waste of time trying to get them to understand the real reason why you're ditching them, because mentally, they're not ready to process such information. If they ever get ready to walk the tightrope of success, they'll understand, but for now, this is all they need to know.

Practice what you are going to say several times before the actual day so you don't miss anything out. If you think you need to, write down some notes and bring them with you. On the day, explain that you brought your notes because you don't want to miss anything out.

Set Boundaries: In some cases, you may not be able to completely cut off the friendship because you work together. The only way to deal with such a situation is to set boundaries about how you want to move forward with the relationship. You could say something like:

"You are such an amazing person. You've helped me through so much since we've been friends. We've had such an awesome time together, and I will be forever grateful for our friendship. We've worked together for five years, and we are friends in and out of work. However, I'm on a different journey at the moment. During my lunch breaks, instead of us hanging out and chatting, I want to spend time listening to educational podcasts or reading. Also, I can't keep up with the partying, constant conversations, texting, and social media engagement. I need to focus on my goals, and that means cutting a lot of things out of my life for the time being, including certain friendships, and unfortunately you're one of them. You haven't done anything wrong; I'm not angry with you, I'm not upset with you, but I just need to devote all my energy towards my goals. What I need from you is for you to stop contacting me altogether. Again, it's not that you've done anything wrong; it's just that I'm going to have tunnel vision for a while, and I'm not sure how long that's going to be. We work together, so I'm not trying to avoid you—of course we can talk when we see each other because we are not enemies. I want the best for you, I really do. I'll call you and let you know all about it when I'm done."

You've now freed yourself from the bondage of having to lie every lunchtime by saying you're going out to run errands when you're really sitting in the car around the corner from your office.

They Might Ask Questions: As much as you think you've explained yourself clearly and that your friend will understand what you've said, accept it, and move on with their life, that most likely won't be the case. People don't give up that easily, especially on something they've invested in. All those hours spent on the phone, going out and going on vacations are seen as investments. They are the things friends do to strengthen their bond. Not only do they like you as a person, but they don't want to feel as if they've wasted years of their life on a friendship that's about to come to an end because you want to work on your goals. Some people are not going to tolerate that and will attempt to convince you that you are making a big mistake. They might ask you questions like:

- "Don't you like me anymore?"
- "What have I done that's made you change your mind about our friendship?"
- "Am I the only one you're dumping? What about all our other friends?"
- "So we can't catch up every now and again to see how things are going?"

- "So you want me to stop calling you altogether?"
- "Are you sure this is a good idea? You're going to be so lonely."
- "Don't you want me to help you with your goals?"

If you get bombarded with questions, be strong, because your friend will make you feel as if you're making a terrible mistake and that there's something wrong with you. Don't let the questions affect you. Stick to your guns and keep the conversation moving. If success is going to become your new normal, you will need to get rid of everything that's holding you back. The reality is that if you plan on making success a lifestyle, you will eventually lose contact with all your friends. But don't worry, because you will make new friends who are on the same level as you. With that being said, in Chapter 12, you'll learn how to make success a lifestyle.

CHAPTER 12:

SUCCESS IS NOT TEMPORARY: HOW TO MAKE SUCCESS A LIFESTYLE

"Without continual growth and progress, such words as improvement, achievement, and success have no meaning."
—Benjamin Franklin

As a child, I remember my mom struggling with her weight; she was always going on one diet or another, and complaining that she wasn't able to maintain her weight loss. But when we were going on vacation, or she had a special event to go to, she would suddenly find the motivation to lose an excessive amount of weight. I found it fascinating that my mother could fluctuate between being extremely fat and extremely slim. I later learned that the reason she couldn't maintain her weight loss was because after she lost the weight, she went right back to consuming an unhealthy diet. The salads were quickly replaced with chips, cookies, and chocolate. The lesson I learned from this was that whatever changes you are trying to make, make it a lifestyle, and not something temporary. Goal attainment should become the norm to you; it should be second nature, like brushing your teeth, not something you do every once in a while. In this chapter, you will learn how to make success a lifestyle.

Why Success Is Not the Norm in Society

Since the beginning of time, society has dictated to us what it means to be successful. Typically, that means the American dream: money in the bank, a nice home, a vacation home, an attractive partner, and 2.4 children. If that's your idea of success, that's okay, but if not, it's important to define success for yourself before you get caught in the conformity trap. To me, success means having the financial freedom to follow your passions, with the main goal of making an impact on the world. Regardless of your definition of success, success is not the norm, because the majority of people don't know how to become successful. Success principles are not taught in schools; therefore, most of us do what we are supposed to do and play it safe: get an education and find a career. However statistics suggest 85% of people hate their jobs. Why is it that following this script rarely leads to success? Here are some possible reasons.

We Don't Know Who We Are: In Chapter 1, we discussed self-awareness, because there is so much more to knowing yourself than naming your likes and dislikes. Self-knowledge is about understanding your own beliefs, values, and behaviors. It's about knowing what motivates and inspires you to become the best version of yourself, and leaning into those things. When you don't know yourself, it's easy to become a victim of the system and just follow the crowd because that's what everyone else is doing. But as I found out, and I'm sure you have too, following the crowd leads you into a dead end. There are several things you will experience when you don't know yourself. These include:

- You hate your job.
- Your decisions are fear-based.
- Your decisions are obligation-based.
- You feel lonely.
- You have bad relationships.
- You allow people to dictate to you.
- You don't know what direction you're taking in life.
- You judge yourself harshly.

You may recognize some of these symptoms, but some of them might be unconscious. As you develop more self-awareness, they will become more apparent to you.

It Destroys Confidence: According to the *Cambridge Dictionary*, conformity means "Behavior that follows the usual standards that are expected by a group or society." While there are many benefits to conformity, it is also extremely harmful because it strips people of their individuality. When a person has been stripped of their individuality, they operate from a place of fear. They become afraid that if they don't follow the norms and standards of society, they will be ostracized by family and friends. Therefore, most people do what is expected of them, even if deep down it is not what they want to do.

I once read a story about a man called Geoffrey who wanted to be an artist, but he came from a family of lawyers, doctors, and engineers, and he was expected to take the same career path. Geoffrey became an engineer; the art that he truly loved was his hobby. He got married, had children, and lived the American dream. From the outside looking in, Geoffrey had the perfect life. But he wasn't happy because he hadn't followed his heart. To Geoffrey, success wasn't about an outward display of wealth; it was about becoming the best version of himself and living his truth. He became so depressed that his wife divorced him, took the kids and everything he owned. It wasn't until he hit rock bottom, was forced into therapy and learned about the consequences of conformity that he became true to himself and followed his passion. During therapy, he discovered that one of the main reasons for his depression was that conformity had destroyed his confidence.

When you have been conditioned to believe that the only way to be accepted is to become someone you are not, you develop the subconscious belief that who you truly are is not good enough. As a result, you never reach your full potential because you have no passion for what you are doing. Geoffrey stated that his wife wanted more out of life—a bigger house, a nicer car, and more vacations. But he had no desire to put in the effort required to get promoted. However, he would lock himself up in his studio and paint for hours. His wife mocked his artwork and couldn't understand why he invested so much into something that wasn't making him any money yet refused to put the same energy into getting promoted at work. Today, Geoffrey has thrown off the cape of conformity and is now a successful artist, with his work showcased in galleries worldwide.

No Financial Education: I don't want to sound like a conspiracy theorist, but I truly believe that the capitalist system we are living in does not benefit anyone other than the people at the top controlling the system. I don't think it is a coincidence that society is set up the way it is. As I've mentioned several times throughout this book, we are told to get an education, find a career, work for 40 years, and retire at 65. By the age of 65, most people are suffering from several health issues, mainly because of how hard they've worked, and spend the rest of their days in and out of hospital. To make matters worse, we don't get to keep the majority of our money because we pay so much tax. This is the nature of capitalism; the rich get richer, and everyone else is just about surviving.

Schools do not teach children about financial literacy because if people knew how to make their money work for them, they would stop working for the system. Without the right knowledge about finances, it's impossible to become successful because you're always going to be stuck in survival mode. A few years ago, I learned about a program called Financial Independence Retire Early (FIRE). Through excessive saving and investment, the program allows people to become millionaires and retire early even if they are working a traditional 9–5 job. To achieve this status, it requires extreme planning, discipline, and wise investment. Thousands of people have managed to retire early because of FIRE. My question is: why isn't this taught in school? Go figure!

How to Make Success a Lifestyle

When you know better, you do better. I didn't acquire this knowledge until I was in my 30s. But now I know what to do, I am teaching others because I know that it works. Success is a lifestyle for me because I've *made* it a lifestyle—and you can too. Here's how:

Develop Good Habits: Good habits are the foundation of making success a lifestyle. Self-discipline is still a challenge for me because I've spent the majority of my life being undisciplined. While I have developed several good habits over the years, they are still not automatic, and sometimes I have to will myself to do them. I look forward to the day when my good habits come as naturally to me as brushing my teeth. I say that because when I wake up in the morning, the first thing I do is walk to the bathroom and brush my teeth. And the last thing I do before I go to bed at night is brush my teeth. That's because I've been trained to brush my teeth twice a day since childhood—and so has the majority of the world. All the bad habits we have, like unhealthy eating, watching too much TV, and scrolling, have developed over time. The good news is that you can develop good habits. But before we get into that, let's gain some more insight into the science of habits.

A habit is an action that you perform repeatedly, and it can be healthy or unhealthy. Good habits will help you develop personally and professionally, and they will help you achieve your goals. But as I discovered, bad habits will slow you down, destroy your health, and make you feel unsatisfied with life. Habits are motivated by our brain's reward system, and there is typically something specific that triggers them. For example, walking past Starbucks and smelling the scent of freshly brewed coffee will entice you to go into the store and buy a cup. Feeling frustrated in your relationship can trigger you to drink more than one glass of wine. After repeating the action many times, it becomes a habit. Here are a few examples of habits.

- Chewing a piece of gum after a meal
- Putting on your seatbelt as soon as you get into a vehicle

- Drinking a cup of tea after work
- Eating sugary foods when you get stressed
- Scrolling through social media during dinner

Habits make the brain more efficient, even if those habits are bad. Positive efficiency is drinking celery juice every morning because the brain knows that your body has a positive reaction to it. Negative efficiency is the brain immediately directing you to the cookie jar when you're stressed because, although it makes you feel better, processed sugary food is unhealthy.

In order to develop good habits, it's important to understand the difference between habits and routine. The main difference is that routines are intentional—you are aware that you are doing them—while habits run on autopilot. Routines require conscious practice or you will stop doing them. On the other hand, habits are not something we typically think about. Back to the example of brushing your teeth; you don't think about it, you just do it. The main reason professional athletes are so good at what they do is that they've developed a habit of practicing. It's something they do every day without thinking about it. Growing up, your parents stopped telling you to brush your teeth and asking whether you had brushed your teeth when they realized it had become a habit. Routines become habits when you start doing them on autopilot. If you want to develop the habit of drinking a healthy smoothie every morning, the moment you go to the kitchen and make one without thinking about it is when it has become a habit.

The author of *The Power of Habit*, Charles Duhigg, states that the foundation of every habit is a process called "the habit loop," which takes place in four stages:

1. **Cue/Trigger:** The mind is always scanning your environment searching for hints about the location of rewards. Once you find the cue, you know you are getting closer to the reward. The brain is then triggered to engage in a certain behavior, and that's when craving begins.

2. **Craving:** Every habit is motivated by cravings. The craving is what drives you to act. However, the habit is not what you're craving; you are craving the *desire*, for how it makes you feel. For example, smokers crave a cigarette because it calms them down or makes them feel relieved. A person addicted to unhealthy food craves a cheeseburger because it makes them feel good when they're eating it.

3. **Response:** When you engage in the habit, that's the response. Nevertheless, the response is dependent upon the level of motivation you have to perform the habit. For example, let's say you have a habit of unhealthy eating, and you are craving a pizza. You have lost your bank card and you only have cash, so you can't order it online. You don't have a car, it's 3:00 a.m., and it will take you 30 minutes to walk to the store. When you weigh up the pros and cons, you come to the conclusion that it's too much effort to put in just for a pizza, so you decide against it and go to bed.

4. **Reward:** The reward is the main goal of any habit. For example, let's say you have a habit of buying donuts anytime you see a bakery. You go into town to run some errands, and you notice a bakery. That's the cue. The

cue triggers the craving of wanting a chocolate-covered donut, and the response is to go inside the bakery, buy the donut and eat it.

We are always seeking rewards because when we indulge in them, our cravings are satisfied.

In a study conducted by the University of London, it was discovered that on average, it takes approximately 66 days to develop a habit. However, some habits took longer than others to form, and in some cases, they took up to 254 days. Additionally, it also depends on the approach taken. For example, it would take longer for a person to give up smoking if they replaced cigarettes with candy instead of a nicotine patch. Also, it depends on how much effort a person is willing to devote to developing the habit, and how motivated they are to change their behavior.

You develop good habits by replacing bad ones. Here are some tips to avoid when making this transition:

Failure to Control Your Environment: As I mentioned earlier, you are more likely to give in to a temptation if it is present. Therefore, take control of your environment by removing temptation. For example, if you want to stop eating junk food, get rid of all your unhealthy snacks and replace them with healthy ones. Also, meal-prep and fill your freezer with ready-made meals so you've always got a home-cooked meal on hand and you're not so tempted to order junk food. If you know you struggle to work from home, go to the library, a coffee shop, or co-working space. If you want to start going to the gym every morning, lay your gym clothes out so they're the first thing you see when you wake up. Controlling your environment will make it a lot easier to develop new habits.

Changing Multiple Habits: Trying to change too many bad habits at once will overwhelm you, so it's best to stick to one at a time. As mentioned, if too much effort is required, you will be less motivated to do it. After you have developed one habit, move on to the next.

Not Committed to Change: Remember it can take up to 254 days to develop a habit, so don't get discouraged when it doesn't happen overnight. It is up to you to commit to the changes you want to see in your life—so, if you're ready to give up after two weeks, this journey is not for you.

Focusing on the Outcome: Developing good habits will help you turn success into a lifestyle. Therefore, don't focus on outcomes; focus on making the goal permanent. For example, instead of setting a goal to save enough money for a new car, set a goal to save a certain percentage of your income every year. Don't be like my mother and only set goals to lose weight for certain events; instead, change your eating habits for life. Eliminate short-term outcomes and focus on long-term goals and changing your behavior permanently.

Refusing to Start Small: Attempting to make drastic changes will always fail because the brain will find it too difficult to adjust. Therefore, don't shy away from small beginnings. While you won't be able to see immediate results, the small changes you make will add up. Stop focusing on the bigger picture, and build up to the end result slowly.

Now it's time to put everything you've just read into practice and start replacing your bad habits with good ones. Here are some tips:

Find the Root Cause: Some bad habits are the result of deep-rooted psychological issues, and the only way to overcome them is by seeking professional help to find the root cause. Here's a story about my friend Jessie. Jessie had been severely overweight for her entire life. She was the bubbly fat kid at school who everyone loved because she came across as so confident, despite the extra pounds she carried. She was one of the bold people who didn't take the traditional route and pursued her dream of owning her own jewelry company. Jessie worked very hard and became a multimillionaire by the age of 21. However, she had one problem—her weight. She tried every new diet that came out, would lose the weight and put it right back on a few weeks later. Jessie desperately wanted to lose the weight and keep it off, but the pull to return to an unhealthy lifestyle was just too strong.

After years of trying, she decided to have therapy. What she discovered was that weight gain was an unconscious defense mechanism. At the age of six, Jessie was molested by her stepfather. Her response to the abuse was to repel men so they were not attracted to her. According to society (this is not my opinion, guys), men are not attracted to overweight women. Additionally, she didn't wear any makeup, kept her hair short, and wore baggy clothes to hide her weight. At 28, Jessie had never had a boyfriend—which was a sign that her unconscious desire to repel men worked. After working through her issues with the therapist, Jessie lost the weight and kept it off.

I said all that to say this: for those of you seriously struggling to break certain habits but unable to pinpoint the root of the problem, I would advise that you see a therapist. One of my bad habits was coming home from work and sitting in front of the television for the rest of the night. If I wasn't watching something, I was scrolling through social media or talking on the phone. While it's normal for people to watch TV after work, it becomes destructive when you are glued to the television for the entire night. When I evaluated my life to find out where this habit came from, I realized that was what my parents did when I was a kid. My dad always came home from work first, he would go upstairs, use the bathroom, and take off his tie. Then he would come downstairs, fix a plate of food, and watch TV for the rest of the night. Back then there was no social media, but if he wasn't watching something, he was sitting in front of the television talking on the phone. When my mom came home from work, she would do exactly the same thing. My parents didn't have any ambitions, and I never saw them do anything other than go to work and watch television, and so that became my norm. When I moved into my own place, I did exactly the same thing. Once I discovered that this was learned behavior, and that it was not the norm, it became easier for me to overcome it. Do some digging and find out what habits of yours are learned behaviors.

Eliminate Triggers: Identify all the triggers connected to your bad habit and eliminate them. This could be places, people, and activities. One of the reasons developing good habits was such a long process for me was because I kept letting the wrong people into my life. After taking an extended break from dating, I met a really nice young lady whom I connected with because she was also into personal development. However, she was still eating a terrible diet, and anytime she would come over, I would give in to her demands to order a takeout. Eventually, I had to end the relationship because she was a trigger. When she was with me, my diet was terrible; when she wasn't, it was great. If you are serious about breaking bad habits, get rid of all triggers, including people.

Reduce Cravings: Cravings are about inducing a specific feeling, which means you can reduce cravings by engaging in a healthy habit to induce that same feeling. For example, if you smoke to feel relaxed, do something healthy to help you feel relaxed, such as deep-breathing exercises. Or maybe you drink several cups of coffee throughout the day to feel more energized and alert; replace the coffee with an energy-boosting drink such as a green smoothie.

Create a Routine: In Chapter 9, you learned about the importance of a morning routine. I'm mentioning it again here because repetition is how you develop healthy habits. By making a conscious decision to do the same thing every day, it will eventually become your new normal. To keep track of your progress, start with a 30-day challenge. I mentioned this in Chapter 3, but it is also very useful when you are trying to develop a new habit. Whatever your new habit is, write it at the top of a sheet of paper, and the numbers 1–30 underneath it. Stick the sheet of paper in a location where you will see it every day. I stuck mine above my light switch. Every morning, after I had finished my routine, I used a red marker to cross out a number. The goal is to complete 30 consecutive days. If you miss one day, you've got to start again. After 30 days, start again—don't take a break; just continue where you left off. Whether it takes you 30 days or 254 days, keep it up until the behavior becomes automatic, and then start working on a new habit.

Keep Setting Goals: Your main goal should be to keep getting better in life, and the only way to do this is to keep setting goals. I had already decided on my second book before I had finished writing my first. Partway through writing my second book, I decided to write a three-part series. I then wrote a five-year plan for my book-writing journey. Here are a few reasons why it's important to keep setting goals:

- **Purpose and Direction:** Before I started taking my life seriously, I was just wandering aimlessly through life with no direction. Apart from going on vacation, meeting up with friends and going to the bar, there was nothing to be excited about, and life had no meaning. I admired but at the same time was extremely envious of passionate people because I wanted what they had. But I didn't know how to get it. However, when I started setting goals for myself, it gave me a clear sense of purpose, and I had something productive to focus on. I became concerned with the impact my books were going to make on my readers, and I wanted to do everything in my power to ensure that impact was a good one. Now, my life isn't just about me—it's about helping others. And I think that's the biggest blessing of all.

- **Focus and Motivation:** I remember the first email I received from a lady who had read my book. She wrote with such enthusiasm about how my book was exactly what she needed—how she had implemented everything she had learned, and how it had changed her life. At that point, I had sold no more than 100 books, and I was getting discouraged that I hadn't become the successful author I had envisioned. But that email reminded me why I had embarked on this journey, and it motivated me to keep going. While I hadn't achieved financial success, I was making an impact, and although it was just one person, one person was more than enough.

- **Personal Growth:** With every goal you achieve, you will learn more about yourself and keep getting better. I make sure that every new goal that I set is more difficult than the last because I want to challenge myself. My goals push me out of my comfort zone and force me to learn new skills. I view challenges as opportunities for learning and growth. I enjoy the transformative process that takes place and what I learn about myself once I have achieved the goal. Goal-setting is exciting because I know I will continue to improve as I grow old. I once believed that growing old was a curse, but now I look forward to the person I am training myself to become in my senior years.

Continuous Learning: When I was in college, I did just enough reading to get my degree, and after college I stopped reading altogether. As I stated in Chapter 11, I bought books I hoped would teach me how to get rich quick, but I would read a chapter or two and put the book down when I realized there was going to be more work involved than I was willing to commit to. However, the world is developing at lightning speed. Most people didn't see artificial intelligence (AI) coming; it was almost as if it just popped out of nowhere. But the tech world has been talking about it for years, and those who are committed to continuous learning were not surprised when it became popular. Many industries are being taken over by AI, and reports suggest that by 2025, it will have replaced 85 million jobs worldwide. You will never be caught off guard when you know what's going on—which is one of the many reasons why continuous learning is so important.

I used to get frustrated when people with less experience than me were promoted to management positions before me.

When the opportunity arose, I always applied because I wanted more money and I believed I was qualified because of the length of time I had worked in the industry. However, what I *wasn't* doing was learning new skills and keeping up to date on industry trends. The people who were getting promoted were going to networking events, taking courses, and doing the work required to become the experts the organization needed to take it to the next level.

Continuous learning does to the mind what food does to the body; it nourishes it. You are going to need a nourished mind if you are going to make success a lifestyle. Once I started making money from book sales, I decided to go into real estate, so I spent a year taking courses and reading about it. Today, I have a property portfolio worth millions. At the moment, I'm learning about starting franchises, and I aim to get into that next year. Continuous learning will ensure that you are never left behind.

Like-Minded People: In Chapter 11, we discussed how your friends can hinder your success and how you become like the people you associate with the most. If you want success to become a lifestyle, surround yourself with like-minded people who are constantly working to become the best versions of themselves. Motivational speaker Tony Robbins said, "The only thing that will change your life, change your business, change your relationship, is that you must raise your standards." I got rid of negative friends because they were not adding anything to my life. They were draining my energy and making me feel as if there was something wrong with me for wanting to live the life I knew I deserved. When you surround yourself with people who you can learn from, who encourage you and push you to become the person you were destined to be, it's a joy to be around them.

You feel energized and fired up when in their presence and you leave them feeling even more confident that you are more than capable of achieving your goals. When I started making changes, I felt bored when I was with my old friends. Their conversations no longer interested me, and when I left them, I felt frustrated, irritated, and aggravated. Those feelings were a clear sign that it was time to move on—and that's exactly what I did.

While I did the work to get where I am today, one of the reasons my life has improved so much is because of who I associate with. I intentionally sought out successful people to befriend. In fact, despite me being extremely successful, I am the least successful person in my friendship group. My friends challenge me to aim for greater heights because they know I am capable. However, as Tony Robbins stated, I had to raise my standards to find these people. I had to be very intentional about who I chose to associate with. And it worked in my favor; I no longer deal with jealousy, envy, and having to explain why I'm so dedicated to what I'm doing. I see most of my new friends four times a year, and we catch up on the phone once a month. We don't bombard each other with text messages and phone calls several times a day, and we are not concerned about social media. We all understand that time is our greatest asset, and we don't waste it on fruitless endeavors. We understand that if we want to achieve our goals, we've got to work at achieving them. And that's the beauty of surrounding yourself with like-minded people—you all get it! Here are some of the characteristics you should look out for when searching for your new friend group:

- **Hard Workers:** As mentioned, my former friends and I were obsessed with get-rich-quick schemes. We wanted the wealth, but we didn't want to do the work required to get it. If we had invested the same amount of time and energy into working to achieve our goals instead of looking for the easy route, we would have all become successful. You don't get what you want out of life sitting on your backside dreaming about it. You get out of life what you put into it, and the harder you work, the more you will get. It's that simple. Hard work is not a natural human trait; we desire comfort more than anything else—which is why I wanted to take the easy route to success. But there *is* no easy route; it doesn't exist. Unless you win the lottery, you are not going to become financially free overnight. And even then, research suggests that 70% of lottery winners lose their wealth within a few years of cashing in on the winning ticket because, instead of learning about how to invest their money and make it work for them, they spend it. Hard work must become your new normal, and one way to ensure you don't slip back into old habits is to have friends who are equally as hardworking as you.

- **Smart People:** If you were to ask the average person to describe a smart person, nine times out of ten, they will refer to someone who is college-educated and has a good career. While I'm not knocking traditional education, it doesn't necessarily make you smart. The most intelligent people I know don't have a college degree; some of them dropped out of high school to follow their dreams. Over the years, I've learned that there is more to intelligence than having a high IQ. Smart people are knowledge seekers; they are also seeking new information to gain a deeper understanding about life.

They are critical thinkers, problem solvers; they possess excellent communication skills and social awareness. Smart people seek to get the best out of life, and they don't waste time about it. These are the people you should connect with.

- **Positive Thinkers:** Positive thinkers are fully aware that we live in a negative world, but they have chosen to filter out the negativity and focus on the positive aspects of life. Although negative thinking was once the norm for me and my friends, when I think back to those days, it was an extremely depressing time. I felt as if there was no hope and that I would never have the life that I desired. I had no idea I could *create* the life I wanted by changing my thoughts. While it was my responsibility to control my thoughts, I was heavily influenced by my friends. Because we only focused on what we could see, and we didn't like what we could see, we spent all our time complaining about our inability to acquire what we wanted. However, my new friends choose to focus on what they *can* do to improve their lives. If they are not satisfied with something, they change it instead of focusing on what they don't like. It's a very simple philosophy but difficult to implement when you are surrounded by the wrong people.

- **Visionaries and Dreamers:** Visionaries and dreamers are rare people with a very unique outlook on life. They are constantly looking into the future, they always have new ideas, and are always working to turn their dreams into a reality. The average person can't understand them because they do not conform to the norms and values of society, and, as mentioned, are often incorrectly labeled as crazy or odd. However, if there were no visionaries or dreamers in this world, it would never move forward. Think about it for a moment; everything you own was created by a visionary—from the bed you sleep in, to the shoes you wear, and the laptop you use every day. These creations were first formed in the inventor's mind; it was an invisible idea. And then they did the work required to turn it into a reality. But since they were extraordinary, rare people, I suspect their ideas were not celebrated when they excitedly explained them to their friends.

To avoid being harshly criticized for daring to think outside the box, search for friends who are visionaries and dreamers and will join in with your excitement when you tell them about your next big idea. They won't ridicule you and accuse you of being too ambitious because of the goals you have set for yourself.

Success is a very difficult journey, and there is nothing comfortable about it. You will be misunderstood, your friends and family will judge you unfairly, and the work you'll need to do to turn your dreams into a reality will be exceptionally hard. Professional athletes love performing their sport of choice, but they don't enjoy training. The interesting thing is that they train more than they compete. LeBron James trains six days a week and is out of bed at 5:00 a.m. to get to his workout sessions. I am sure he'd rather be in bed, but he knows that if he's going to maintain his physique in order to play the way that he does, he's got to defeat the temptation to hit the snooze button. Professional athletes have embraced discomfort, because they understand that growth only happens outside your comfort zone. And that's what we are going to talk about next.

CHAPTER 13:

EMBRACING DISCOMFORT: GET COMFORTABLE WITH BEING UNCOMFORTABLE

> *"You can choose courage or you can choose comfort. You cannot have both."*
>
> —Brené Brown

In a room packed with 2000 people, I said, "Raise your hand if any of you here likes feeling uncomfortable." Not one person raised their hand—and I wasn't expecting anyone to because it is human nature to want to remain in your comfort zone. Stepping outside of it, and entering into new territory is terrifying. The brain is even designed to protect you from being uncomfortable. That's why it's so difficult to break bad habits. The subconscious mind programs us to behave in a certain way, but the problem is that the subconscious mind is subjective, and it doesn't reason or think independently. It simply follows the commands given to it by the conscious mind. This would be great if we were programmed to behave in ways that benefit us, but the majority of us aren't. Therefore, when we attempt to step out of our comfort zone, the subconscious mind fights the new information being received, in order to keep us bound to our old behavioral patterns. But without discomfort, there is no growth. This is just as true physically as it is mentally. When a baby's teeth are coming through, the gums become very painful, and the baby bites things to soothe the discomfort. Or for those wanting to change their body, they won't see a transformation unless they lift heavy weights that cause their muscles to become sore.

When I said, "Raise your hand if any of you here want to become successful," every single person in the room raised their hand. Again, I wasn't surprised; I knew the results I would get before asking the questions. But I also knew that the majority of people in the room would never achieve the success they desired because they were not willing to step out of their comfort zone long enough to see results. And no, I'm not being pessimistic; the statistics prove that, even when people know what to do to become successful, they don't do it because they don't have the drive to. Don't be one of those people. Dare to push yourself to the limit and you'll be amazed at what you can achieve.

What Is the Comfort Zone?

In the tenderness of your comfort zone, life feels familiar and safe, and for most of you, finding the motivation to leave is extremely difficult. But the longer you remain in your comfort zone, the more opportunities you will miss, and the harder it will become to achieve your goals. It takes a changed mindset and an exceptional amount of willpower to get out of and *stay* out of your comfort zone. Let's take a look at what the comfort zone is and why most of us find it so challenging to break out of it.

When you are not being challenged or tested, psychologically you feel at ease because your mind is not resisting anything. In fact, you feel pretty good. This is your comfort zone. When a person is inside their comfort zone, they don't participate in new experiences or activities that they are not familiar with because it makes them feel as if they are not in control of their environment. Your comfort zone protects you from feelings of stress, anxiety, and pain. There is an atmosphere of uncertainty when a person steps outside their comfort zone, and that uncertainty makes us feel anxious. It is human nature to avoid these negative feelings. The brain is actually hardwired that way. Here are some of the main reasons we are afraid to step out of our comfort zone:

- **Uncertainty and Fear:** While you might have a vision in your head of what you want to achieve, fear of the unknown can prevent you from achieving it if you let it. Change scares people because they don't know what they're giving up. When you become very accustomed to the way you live, even if it's unhealthy, the thought of anything else doesn't appeal to you.

- **The Desire for Comfort:** As the saying goes, "Better the devil you know than the devil you don't." In other words, some people would rather stay in a bad situation they are familiar with than get out and venture into something unfamiliar. The fear is that the new situation will be worse. But that's the problem with fear—it's not fact. You really have no idea what it will be like on the other side of your fear. The reality is that that's where you need to be: on the other side of your fear.

The Benefits of Stepping Out of Your Comfort Zone

Author Neale Donald Walsch said, "Life begins at the end of your comfort zone." In other words, when we step outside our comfort zone, we experience something we wouldn't have had we remained in our familiar and safe world. One of the greatest feelings I experienced when I stepped out of my comfort zone was after I did a bungee jump. I'm absolutely terrified of heights, but the adrenaline rush I experienced afterwards was indescribable. From that moment onwards, I felt like I could conquer the world. There are unlimited rewards for those brave enough to venture out of their comfort zone. Here are some of them:

Resilience: According to the American Psychological Association (APA), "Resilience is having the emotional, mental, and behavioral flexibility to adjust to both external and internal demands." It is the ability to bounce back from adversity with a renewed sense of purpose. Instead of a person allowing what they went through to hinder them, they use it as fuel to turn it into something positive. People are not born with resilience; it's a skill that is developed, sometimes intentionally, sometimes unintentionally. One way to develop resilience is by stepping out of your comfort zone. By putting yourself in uncomfortable situations, you develop the mental strength required to overcome challenges in your professional and personal life.

Confidence: To step outside your comfort zone, you need confidence. The more you do this, the more confidence you will develop. Stepping outside your comfort zone is about facing your fears. For example, I used to hate public speaking; the idea of speaking in front of a group of people all staring at me struck so much terror into me and I had no desire to confront this fear. However, when I started working on stepping outside my comfort zone, I decided to try public speaking. Although I was extremely nervous, I learned that it actually wasn't that bad, and I felt a lot more confident about speaking in front of an audience. The more public speaking I did, the better I became at it. The more you step outside your comfort zone, the more your confidence will grow.

Self-Actualization: Self-actualization is when a person reaches the pinnacle of life and becomes who they were destined to be. According to Abraham Maslow's Hierarchy of Needs, self-actualization is the highest level of psychological development. Unfortunately, most people never reach this level. There are several reasons for this, but one of them is that they never step outside their comfort zone. If you remain in your comfort zone, it's impossible to discover your true potential. However, once you push through this fear, you'll develop a strong desire to learn more about yourself, and you'll start seeking out opportunities to develop your potential. However, it's important to understand that there is no end goal when it comes to self-actualization; it's a journey of continuous growth. Basically, you make a conscious decision to keep developing yourself until you take your last breath.

Less Regrets: Author Bronnie Ware wrote a book called *The Top Five Regrets of the Dying*. During her research, she discovered that the palliative care patients she interviewed had several life regrets, and there was a common theme amongst them. These included:

- "I wish I was brave enough to tell people how I really felt."

- "I wish I had made more of an effort to be happier."

- "I wish I was brave enough not to live the life that others expected of me, and to have been true to myself."

Ware states that those who failed to live their dreams and settled for mediocracy experienced a deep regret for the things they didn't do. Also, those who refused to break bad habits but convinced themselves that was just the way they were, and that they were incapable of change also had deep regrets and wished they had made more of an effort to change their reality.

While you'll most likely live an easier life if you play it safe and never leave your comfort zone, it won't be fulfilling. You will never experience the joy of self-actualization, knowing that you've done everything in your power to become the person you know you were created to be.

How to Embrace Discomfort

A study conducted by psychologists John Dodson and Robert Yerkes discovered a strong relationship between anxiety and performance. The experiment involved getting mice to find their way through a maze. The mice were more motivated to do so when they were given slight electric shocks. But when the shocks were too strong, the mice became fearful and began to hide. The psychologists named the phenomenon the Yerkes-Dodson Law. It stipulated that a small amount of anxiety or pressure boosts performance. But when it's too much, it causes panic. This law explains why chronic procrastinators can complete a project three days before the deadline, despite being given a month to do it. However, if they miss the deadline, panic sets in and they're forced to ask for more time.

Basically, trying to step too far outside your comfort zone has the same effect. Engaging in activities that make you feel extremely anxious will have you quickly running back into your comfort zone. So, the most effective way to leave it is to do so gradually until you find that good level of stress. If you are ready to step out of your comfort zone, here are some tips to get you started:

Try Something New: Learning a new skill is a great way to step outside of your comfort zone without feeling too much pressure. Growing up, I had always wanted to play the piano, but my parents couldn't afford lessons, so I scrapped the idea. One day, years later, I was walking through the mall, and there was a man sitting in the corner playing the keyboard so beautifully. It reminded me that I had always wanted to play the piano, so I booked myself some lessons. I knew I wasn't going to be any good at it, but I was okay with that—I was willing to learn. I actually enjoyed the process of learning, practicing, and growing because it helped boost my confidence. To get started with embracing discomfort, think about something you've always wanted to do—and do it. It could be traveling solo, skydiving, public speaking, or attending a networking event.

Change Your Routine: In Chapter 8, I talked about the importance of establishing a daily routine, and I stand by that. But once you have developed a routine, you will have settled into your comfort zone. You can break out of this by changing your routine and making it more challenging. You don't need to do much, because, as mentioned, if you attempt to step *too far* out of your comfort zone, you'll make yourself too anxious and will give up. Therefore, changing your routine might be as simple as waking up earlier than usual. For example, if you wake up at 5:00 a.m., start waking up at 4:30 a.m. Or if you work out for 45 minutes, work out for an hour. The aim is to push yourself past your normal limits so you can keep growing.

Embrace Failure: One of the reasons people remain in their comfort zone is that they are afraid of failure. They don't want to apply for the promotion in case they don't get it. They don't want to attempt to lose weight in case they don't reach their target. And they don't want to start their own business in case it isn't successful. The problem with this mindset is that you will never step out of your comfort zone and achieve anything worthwhile because you'll allow the fear of failure to hold you back. However, when you change your perspective about fear and see it as a learning opportunity instead of a closed door, you'll develop the confidence required to achieve your dreams. The reality is that failure only exists if you allow it to. You fail when you give up—so, unless you give up, you can never fail. But every time you don't get it right, you can try something new until, eventually, you achieve your goal. People who embrace failure enjoy challenges because they understand that on the other side of that challenge is growth.

Embrace Your Fears: If you were not afraid of the things you were afraid of, what would you do with your life? Skydive? Start a business? Break up with your partner? Or start a public-speaking career? Instead of running away from your fears, run *towards* them—because everything you've ever wanted is on the other side of fear. Here are some tips on how to embrace your fears:

- **Reframe Fear:** Reframing your fear allows you to turn something crippling into something motivating.

For example, despite the fact that I've given hundreds of speeches, I still experience some level of fear before I get on stage. But I remind myself that fear is a natural emotion and it's my body's way of preparing me to do my best. This thought process doesn't fail me, and I always do a fantastic job.

- **Change Your Language:** The reason your friends and family know you as the person who fears XYZ is because you probably wear your fear on your sleeve, and you're always talking about it. Even when you're alone, you speak to yourself about your fears. Changing your language surrounding fear isn't about denying your fear; it's about acknowledging that constantly reminding yourself that you're afraid of something reinforces the fear, which doesn't serve you. Therefore, instead of saying, "I'm terrified of heights," say, "I am going to overcome my fear of heights."

- **Breathe:** One of the reasons Navy SEALs can go into dangerous situations with such confidence is because of their breathing techniques. It helps them stay focused and calm, and in many cases, it's what keeps them alive. One of the most popular breathing techniques used by the Navy SEALs is the 4-7-8 breathing technique. It goes like this:
    - Counting to four, take a deep breath in.
    - Hold the breath for seven seconds.
    - Breathe out completely while counting to eight.
    - Continue until you feel calm.

I do this breathing exercise for half an hour before my speaking engagements, and it works, guys—it really takes the edge off and makes you feel more confident.

    I wish I could tell you that success is smooth sailing and that you're going to achieve your goals immediately, but I can't because that's not how success works. Even those born with a silver spoon in their mouth whose parents funded their visions will still encounter disappointment along the way. Whether it's people letting you down, or things not turning out the way you had hoped, you will experience many failures on this journey. As painful as it is, my plea to you is to not give up when the going gets tough, because it's often when it appears as if it's never going to happen that your breakthrough shows up. The key is to develop the resilience required to stay in the game when all hell is breaking loose around you. Let's continue this conversation in Chapter 14.

CHAPTER 14:

DEALING WITH DISAPPOINTMENT: THE POWER OF PATIENCE

"Disappointment is a temporary detour on the road to success."

—Zig Ziglar

We've all felt disappointment when things don't happen the way we planned, whether a romantic relationship we thought was going well came to an end, or we didn't get the promotion we spent so much time preparing for. When life sends us a curveball, it's important that we learn how to deal with it because disappointment is something we will all face at some point. When my first book didn't do well, I can't even begin to describe how disappointed I was. I had spent months writing the book, speaking positive affirmations about success, and visualizing the moment I got a notification that my book was a number one bestseller. But that didn't happen. Despite the amount of marketing and preparation I had done, the book didn't even sell 100 copies. I felt like I had wasted time and money on a dream that was never going to materialize. But what kept me going was reading about other people's success stories and how they had persevered, despite having so many setbacks. Developing resilience and patience was a part of the process. I had to keep going, and that's exactly what I did. As you embark on this journey of taking the action required to achieve your goals, you are going to experience many disappointments along the way. How you handle them will determine your success.

What Is Disappointment?

As I've stated, we are all familiar with disappointment, but it's a lot deeper than we think because of how it relates to our emotions in general. According to the *Oxford Dictionary*, disappointment means "The unhappiness or discouragement that results when your hopes or expectations have not been satisfied, or someone or something is not as good as you had hoped or expected." Research suggests that humans experience six basic emotions: joy, sadness, anger, surprise, disgust, and fear. In the 1980s, psychologist Robert Plutchik added anticipation and trust to these basic emotions when he developed the Wheel of Emotions theory. The theory states that human emotions are a lot more complex than the basic emotions when experienced in combination with each other. We can also experience emotions such as awe, admiration, aggressiveness, boredom, and annoyance. Disappointment is one of these combinations that is experienced due to sadness. It's what we feel when we don't get the results we were expecting or when someone lets us down. Disappointment can be a mixture of several emotions such as grief, anger, and bitterness.

How to Deal with Disappointment

Since you are going to experience disappointment at some point, it's important that you learn how to deal with it so it doesn't overwhelm you. Here are some tips:

Acknowledge It: The first step in dealing with disappointment is to acknowledge that you are disappointed. Disappointment is an emotion, and it's essential that your emotions are managed effectively or they will overwhelm you. One of the things emotionally unavailable people do to avoid confronting their emotions is to have no expectations. They completely block out any ideas or thoughts about how they think something could turn out. But that's not a healthy way of handling disappointment—so do this instead:

- **Validate It:** After my third book flopped, I just wanted the ground to open up and swallow me because I was so tired of losing. It was so painful that, for a while, I attempted to minimize, ignore, and distract myself from the uncomfortable feelings. Eventually I got myself together and acknowledged how I was feeling, but it was hard. Validating your feelings means calling the emotion out by name and accepting that it's there, because that's how you feel at the moment. Validating your feelings is also about remembering that it's normal to feel the way you feel. There's absolutely nothing wrong with being disappointed because things haven't turned out as you'd hoped. All emotions are valid—the happy and the sad ones.

- **Ride the Wave:** Sometimes I would try and make my emotions disappear by focusing on something else. But that's just another avoidance tactic that will come back to bite you in the butt. Emotions are temporary; they don't last and will remain until they pass. If you've ever watched a surfer in action, they will ride a wave until it disappears. Do the same with your disappointment—ride it until it disappears. Be kind to yourself during this time by reminding yourself that it's normal to feel disappointed that your situation didn't turn out the way you wanted it to.

- **Adjust Your Expectations:** Adjusting your expectations doesn't mean your dream is too big and you need to downsize. When I wrote my first book, I was convinced it would become a bestseller. I had it on my vision board and I was very confident that it would manifest. But it didn't. I was tempted to throw my hands up in despair and give up. During that time, the only thing I was convinced about was that my dream was a fantasy, and I was living in some weird alternate reality that only existed in my mind. Once the disappointment had passed and my mind was clear enough to start strategizing again, one of the things I decided to do was adjust my expectations about becoming a bestseller. I held on to the goal but didn't put a timeframe on it. It would happen when it happened. Once I accepted that, a huge weight was lifted off my shoulders. Every time I released a book, I didn't get on my knees and beg the gods to make me a bestseller this time. I kept writing and waited patiently. I knew it would be my turn one day; and lo and behold, I became a bestseller with the release of my fourth book! So, whatever you are hoping for, adjust your expectations about it, but don't stop working on the goal. For example, let's say you've set a goal to lose 50 lbs within a year, but you hit a wall and the pounds are not dropping off as fast as they were when you started. There's one month left until the end of the year and you still need to lose 20 lbs. Instead of accepting defeat, remove your deadline and keep working on losing weight. Try different techniques and strategies until you reach your desired weight.

Reframe It: We all have defining moments in our lives, and some of them are marked by disappointment. When viewed from the right perspective, these defining moments can work in our favor and help us become more resilient. Winston Churchill, the former prime minister of the United Kingdom, experienced many disappointments during his tenure. One of them happened at the beginning of his career during the First World War. Churchill put together a very unsuccessful military campaign that killed thousands of soldiers, and he was forced to resign from his role as First Lord of the Admiralty. He was so humiliated that he took a break from politics altogether and became an infantry officer. At first, Churchill was so depressed that he named his experience, "Black dog of depression." However, after much thought, he came to the conclusion that it was best to reframe his disappointments into something positive.

Whether you agree with his political stance or not, one can't help but respect how he handled the situation. I mean, thousands of people lost their lives because of the decisions he made; how he didn't completely lose his mind is beyond me.

Unfortunately, most people don't deal with disappointment like this. Instead, they view negative life circumstances through the lens of personal failure. They become obsessed with self-blame and feel humiliated or ashamed that they didn't live up to their high standards. They become angry with themselves and internalize it. Whatever happened, they start believing they deserved it because of their perceived shortcomings. Some people will alleviate the disappointment by pointing the finger at others, which will eventually lead to bitterness, vindictiveness, and doing things to spite those they feel are responsible for their disappointment. Both reactions keep the person trapped in a web of disappointment. Holding on to disappointment is just as unhealthy as refusing to acknowledge it.

Faith-Filled People: We talked about the importance of having the right friends in Chapter 11. In times of disappointment it's even more important to be surrounded by the right people. You see, disappointment isn't final. Just because things have not happened the way you expected, it doesn't mean it's the end, that you should bury your dreams and forget about trying to achieve your goals. When my first book failed, my friends at the time told me to quit; they knew it wasn't going to work out because "normal people" like us don't become successful authors. I don't believe they were trying to be intentionally mean, but words of encouragement were not in their vocabulary. They were used to accepting defeat. In their opinion, the first obstacle was evidence that it wasn't meant to be, so I really couldn't expect anything more from them. What you need in a crisis are people who understand faith. Please understand that faith-filled people are not "yes-people." They are not telling you what they think you want to hear. They are speaking from a position of power. Listen; it takes a certain kind of person to understand faith. They're the "crazy" people we talked about earlier, the ones who refuse to give up on working on something invisible until it turns into something tangible. *These* are the people you want to be around when your hard work isn't materializing because they know how incredibly difficult it is to achieve your goals. They understand the process—that it's not going to happen overnight, that there will be bumps in the road, and that there will be times when you will feel like giving up. You will be able to cry on their shoulders and express your disappointment, but these friends won't allow you to remain in the valley. They will remind you that you have something exceptionally important to achieve, and that it's imperative that you get back in the race.

Develop More Patience: *"One moment of patience may ward off great disaster. One moment of impatience may ruin a whole life."* ~Chinese Proverb. There are many keys to success, and patience is one of them. But patience is a discipline that many of us lack, and it's becoming harder and harder for us to master due to the digital era we are currently living in. Today, everything is available to us at the click of a button. You can do your weekly grocery shopping online and have it delivered to you within an hour. If you want to read a book, you can download it on Kindle within a few seconds. If you want to watch your favorite TV show, listen to a nostalgic song—all of these things are just a click away. While these technological conveniences make life a lot easier, they've also got us used to instant gratification and made us a lot less patient. We are constantly exposed to viral social media posts and YouTube sensations, which make it appear as if these people received overnight success. But is overnight success really a thing? Most successful people would say no. While a product, business, or influencer might appear to be an overnight success, what actually happened was that its or their value suddenly became apparent to consumers. But those same consumers did not see the years of dedication, hard work, relationship-building, disappointments, and having to change strategies it took to gain the attention required for success.

The parable of the Chinese bamboo tree highlights this idea perfectly. A Chinese farmer planted a bamboo tree because he had been told that it would bring miracles to the family of the person who planted the tree. The farmer was excited about the tree, and every day he carefully tended to it by watering and fertilizing it. After one year, he hadn't seen any difference in the soil; there was no growth. So, in year two, he continued watering and fertilizing the tree. Still he saw no growth. But despite his disappointment, the farmer had faith that one day, he would witness a miracle.

In the fifth year, his patience started dwindling and he was about to give up. But one day, he noticed that the seeds had started sprouting, and so he continued watering and fertilizing the tree. Within six weeks, the bamboo tree grew over 60 feet! That in itself seems like a miracle, doesn't it? But is that what really happened? Did the bamboo tree just start growing in the fifth year? Not at all. The tree was growing beneath the surface, but the farmer couldn't see it. Nature knew that the tree was going to grow 60 feet and it needed a strong root system to support how tall it would eventually grow. Without such a strong root system, the bamboo tree would have eventually collapsed. Furthermore, if you know anything about bamboo trees, you'll know that trying to uproot them is virtually impossible. They can survive under any circumstances. The story of the bamboo tree is a reminder that there is no such thing as overnight success, and that you will eventually reap the benefits of patience, perseverance, and faith.

People love hearing success stories because they are rare—and they are rare because most people give up when they do not see any progress or are encountering too many obstacles. In this microwave society that we live in, where we are obsessed with instant gratification, we expect immediate results. People don't value hard work—they want everything now. And life doesn't work like that. During your pursuit of success, you will experience many disappointments. Imagine how the farmer felt every day, week after week, month after month, and year after year putting all his time and energy into a bamboo tree that wasn't growing. He would have been terribly disappointed. But he had the patience to persevere, and it paid off. Here are some tips on how to develop more patience:

- **Identify Your Triggers:** A trigger is something that brings on an unexpected or intense emotional response. Or it can cause a flashback to a trauma that happened in the past. Triggers are typically people, places, or things, but they can also be sensory stimuli. Triggers are typically non-threatening; it's the *reaction* they cause that's the problem. Identifying your triggers is an effective way to help you develop more patience because you'll learn how to react when these triggers show up. Here are some tips on how to identify your triggers:
    - **Your Feelings:** The next time you feel impatient, write down why you feel that way. Pay attention to these feelings when you experience them, especially if they just sneak up on you and are unrelated to the situation.
    - **Listen to Yourself:** Venting about something helps you identify your triggers, because whatever hap-

pened made you feel impatient for a reason. Venting gives you the opportunity to dig a little deeper and discover the underlying issues associated with your situation.

- **Conversations:** Pay attention to the conversations you have with friends and family. Are there topics that evoke strong feelings that challenge your patience? When I practiced this exercise, I learned that talking about success stories was a trigger for me. They frustrated me because I didn't have my own success story, and in many ways I felt like it was never going to happen for me.

• **Observe Patient People:** Successful people are interesting because they are both extremely patient and extremely impatient. They know how to take their time working on a project because their vision of the end result motivates them to continue working on it. However, when it comes to dealing with certain types of people, they have zero patience for them. My mentor Justin is the most successful person I know; he is a commercial real estate developer worth millions. However, I've seen him fire more people than I can count because they got one small thing wrong. His argument is always the same, and it makes perfect sense: "How you do anything is how you do everything" is his response when I attempt to justify why he should keep them on the payroll. But Justin has been in the business for decades, and he understands human nature better than anyone else I know. He says that if you allow them to slack once, they'll keep slacking and destroy your business.

Justin also believes that firing someone for something so minor will force them to examine themselves so they don't make the same mistake on their next job. Other than having no tolerance for anything but excellence, he is a very patient guy. During your observation, you will notice that patient people typically have the following characteristics:

- **Empathy:** *"Empathy is patiently and sincerely seeing the world through the other person's eyes. It is not learned in school; it is cultivated over a lifetime."* ~Albert Einstein. Empathy and patience are deeply connected; you can't have one without the other. As Einstein rightly stated, empathy is about having the ability to see the world from another person's perspective. Patience is about having the ability to wait with a good attitude. Empathetic people are patient because they understand people. While the person without empathy won't have the patience to deal with someone who is a bit slow in certain areas, the empathetic person *will*, because they can understand where they are coming from.

- **Time Management:** Patience boosts productivity because you are better able to organize things in a way that will help you get stuff done. Impatient people like to rush and just get on with it. They have no time to set up systems and processes, and will dive into their projects headfirst without an effective strategy. Pay attention to a patient person, and you will notice how good their time-management skills are. You will rarely catch them rushing around trying to get stuff done because they are always thoroughly organized.

- **Humility:** It takes a lot of humility to be patient. I'll use myself as an example here. When things are not working out as planned, the first thing you want to do is stand on a rooftop or announce on social media why. When my books were failing and people kept asking me what was going on, I played dumb and acted as if everything was going just the way I had planned. However, deep down, I was suffering; I was disappointed, frustrated, and saddened that my dream had not manifested as I had hoped. Nevertheless, I kept writing, despite how I felt. Eventually, the evidence spoke for itself—I became a bestseller and my life completely changed. I left my job and became a full-time author. I bought a bigger house, a nicer car, better clothes. That is the essence of humility: having the patience to wait for something to manifest without feeling the need to prove yourself to everyone during the process.

- **Stress Management:** Patient people don't allow life to stress them out. They understand that life can be stressful, and that there are many things that can cause stress in a person's life, such as family, work, and relationships. But they don't allow stress to control them; *they* control stress by doing the things required to reduce stress in their lives. Additionally, when they do feel stress winding them up, they'll engage in the necessary activities to alleviate it.

- **Practice Acceptance:** Whether you're religious or not, you can't deny the truth in the words from this prayer: "Grant me the serenity to accept the things I cannot change." There are some things you simply don't have any control over and there is absolutely nothing you can do about it. For instance, anytime I published a book, I had no control over how many people bought it. All I could do was write a book that would provide value to the reader, and market the book. I couldn't force anyone to buy it; I could only hope they would. When you learn to accept the things you can't change, your frequency goes up, and you naturally start attracting what you desire. Additionally, you'll be less stressed, frustrated, and anxious because you're no longer putting effort and energy into things that may or may not generate the outcome you desire. Here are a few tips on how to practice acceptance:
  - **Identify:** When you find yourself stressing out about something, identify whether it's something you can control. Get a pen and a notepad and take a seat. Calm yourself down by taking several deep breaths, and then draw a line down the middle of the page. On one side write the word "situation"; on the other side write "How I can control it." You can determine whether you can control a situation by coming up with at least one way to get the outcome you desire. For example, if you're stressed because you've just found out that a client may not be able to pay you, there is nothing you can do to get the client to pay you—they either have the money or they don't. In a situation like this, you have no

choice but to accept that you might not get paid. On the other hand, if you are worried because you have a speaking engagement in a couple of weeks and you're nervous about your performance, you can control that by practicing.

- **Mindfulness:** Mindfulness is about being present and focusing on the moment. When you are trying to control stuff, you're mentally reaching into the future to see how you can manipulate the situation. When you find yourself doing this, stop, take a few deep breaths, and bring your thoughts back to the present moment. You can also repeat a mantra such as, "I choose to focus on the things I can control and let go of the things I can't control."

- **Look for Positives:** As the saying goes, "Every cloud has a silver lining." In other words, you can find something positive in everything, no matter how bad it seems. The next time you're struggling to accept that you have no control over a situation, look for the positive aspects of it. For example, you've arranged an outdoor event but, according to the weather report, it's going to rain on that day. It's a no-brainer that you can't control the weather, but what you *can* do is focus on the fact that while you were praying for it *not* to rain, a farmer in another town was praying for it *to* rain because his crops were drying out. It might not be a positive for you, but it's a positive for him. Celebrate that.

- **Detach:** One way to practice acceptance is to detach yourself from the outcome. Detaching yourself from the outcome means you stop trying to create the outcomes you want, and trust the process. When you attach yourself to an outcome, you create a barrier between you and your desires. Detachment allows you to receive whatever is coming your way. For example, let's say you created a product and you've set a goal of selling one million units within the first six months. There are only three outcomes to this goal: you will sell less, more, or the exact number of units you stated. By fixating on this number, you block the possibility of selling more units, and if you sell less than one million, you'll be disappointed. Therefore, detaching yourself from the outcome frees you from the stress of expectations.

- **Embrace Change:** By embracing change, you give yourself room for growth. If there's one thing I've learned over these past few years, it's that change is inevitable—it's going to happen whether you want it to or not. However, when the change happens, we often find ourselves scrambling to get things back to the way they used to be. The whole purpose of change is growth, and if you don't embrace change, you'll never grow.

- **Enjoy the Process:** Enjoying the process is easier said than done, but it gets easier to do after the first time. Once you get to the other side and you look back, you get to put all the pieces of the puzzle together and learn about why you had to endure the things that you did. Once you count how many lessons you learned, you will appreciate the journey. Now you have valuable insight and wisdom into the power of the process, you'll be able to guide yourself and others through it.

- **STOP:** The STOP practice helps boost patience before a difficult situation occurs, or when our emotions get the better of us. This is how it works:
    - **S:** Stop everything and take a long pause.
    - **T:** Take a few deep breaths and focus on your breath as you breathe.
    - **O:** Observe the situation. What's going on internally and externally?
    - **P:** Proceed. After assessing the situation and choosing the right way to handle things, the final step is to take action.

- **Take a Break:** Taking a break might sound like a very simple solution to developing patience, but it works. Stepping back from a project for a while rejuvenates you so that when you get back to it, you have a renewed sense of purpose. Research proves that taking a break from studying refreshes the body and brain and increases your ability to focus and be more productive, plus it increases your energy levels. However, the break must be a purposeful one or you won't receive the same benefits. For example, scrolling through social media or having a gossip session with a friend won't cut it. A purposeful break is something like taking a 20-minute power nap, taking a walk, meditating, listening to soothing music, or doing some stretching exercises. The same applies if you want to take an extended break from your goals. When I was writing my book, I got writer's block, and no matter how hard I tried, I couldn't write anything. So, I went on vacation. My dad owns a cabin in Toronto. There's no TV or distractions out there. I took a weekend trip and did absolutely nothing but read, meditate, and do yoga. It was so refreshing, and when I came back I had plenty of things to write about.

- **Improve Your Listening Skills:** "What the hell has listening skills got to do with patience?" I hear you asking. My response? "A *lot.*" What do you do the most when someone is speaking to you? I want you to think about this for a moment and be honest with yourself. Most people are waiting for the right moment to insert their opinion. You find it extremely annoying when people do this, don't you? But *you* do it all the time. Before the person has even finished speaking, you want to talk about how you've experienced the same thing—and, worse, give your unsolicited advice or finish their sentences. Another thing people do during a conversation is have one ear in and the other ear out. One ear is listening to the person speak, while the other is listening to their own thoughts. You might be thinking about what you're going to eat for lunch or dinner, the laundry you need to do, or the deadline you need to meet. Go on, admit it! I know I used to do this. But I don't feel so bad about it anymore because most people are terrible listeners. Listening is a skill that the average person hasn't mastered, and one of the skills required to be a good listener is patience. You need patience to listen to people because for them to feel heard, it's essential that you allow them to say everything they need to say. Additionally, they may not be the best at articulating themselves, so you'll need to tune in properly to understand what they are saying. Here are some tips on how to be a better listener:

- **Eye Contact:** When you're having a conversation face to face, make eye contact with the person. Don't look around the room or try to eavesdrop on other conversations—give the person your undivided attention. Making eye contact shows you are interested in what they are saying. However, don't go overboard with it or you will make the person feel uncomfortable. Keep your eyes on the person's face, but look them in the eyes every few seconds for a few seconds at a time. It sounds a lot, but as you practice, you'll get used to it. Experts suggest using the triangle method, which involves looking in one eye for a couple of seconds, then the mouth, and then the other eye.

- **Body Language:** Your body language says a lot more than what's coming out of your mouth. Research suggests that 55% of what we say is nonverbal; our tone makes up for 38% of the conversation, and our words make up 7% of what we say. In other words, listen more with your eyes than your ears. For example, it's social etiquette to respond that we are fine when someone asks how we are doing. We expect the other person to give a positive response. But if the person is having a terrible day, you'll see it in their body language. For example, they say they are doing great and give a smile, but the corners of their mouth are turned down and their eyes are downcast. If you're in the right environment, at this point you can make an empathetic gesture such as placing your arm on their shoulder, looking them in the eye and responding, "What's really going on with you?" Your response will give the person the confidence to open up because it's clear that you've been able to see through their mask. The ability to read body language also makes you more likeable because it gives the impression that you are empathetic and easy to talk to.

- **Don't Interrupt:** "Not to cut you off but…" Have you done that before? Although it's extremely rude to interrupt a person when they're speaking, everyone does it. Just so you're clear, interrupting is saying anything when the speaker hasn't finished speaking. So, asking to interrupt is still interrupting. Keep your mouth closed until it's clear that it's your turn to speak.

- **Hold Your Opinion:** Unless the person asks for your opinion, don't give it. One of the main reasons for this is so the speaker relinquishes their right to get offended. If they ask for your opinion, they've got to accept it whether they like it or not, because they asked. However, if they didn't ask, your unwarranted opinion could start an argument. The same applies for advice. Sometimes a person just wants someone to listen to them while they vent. Only give advice if you're asked for it.

- **Express Interest:** No one wants to talk to someone who doesn't seem interested in their conversation. Therefore, make it abundantly clear you're engaged in the discussion by doing things like nodding, changing your facial expressions, and maintaining eye contact.

- **Wait:** When it appears that the person has finished speaking, wait for a couple of seconds before saying anything. This silence might be a bit awkward, but it will help you determine whether it's time to speak. By asking questions like, "Are you done?" or, "Can I say something now?" you might come across as impatient, like you were just waiting for them to finish speaking so you could say your piece. If the speaker doesn't say anything else during the silence, move on to the next stage.

- **Ask Questions:** If you're not sure exactly what was said, or you want to clarify a few things, ask some questions to gather some more information. You can say something like, "When you said XYZ, did you mean XYZ?"

- **Paraphrase:** Repeat what the speaker said in your own words to show that you were listening and understood. It will also give the person the chance to correct you if you have misinterpreted what they said.

• **Play a Sport:** A fun way to develop patience is to learn how to play a sport. There are many sports that require a lot of patience, such as:

- **Baseball:** Patience is the most important trait to have as a ballplayer because baseball is a waiting game. It involves a lot of downtime—waiting for batters, pitchers, and sitting on the bench. Professional baseball player David Sax once said, "The 3 P's of baseball are patience, persistence, and paying your dues."

- **Golf:** The game requires focus, precision, and strategic decision-making. Players have to wait for things such as the right weather conditions, and mastering varying terrains before they can take a shot.

- **Tennis:** Tennis requires a combination of physical endurance, skill, and strategy. It can take a while before a player gets any points, and matches are sometimes extended until a player wins. Waiting for the right moment to take a shot, and managing the challenges that can sometimes crop up during a game all require patience.

- **Fishing:** Fishing involves sitting on the shore waiting for the fish to take the bait. Fishermen are known to sit outside for several hours waiting to catch something.

Nothing happens all at once; success is cumulative, and when you have achieved your goal and you look back, you'll realize how important the little things were. I didn't pay attention to the little things until my mentor explained the importance of celebrating my small wins. The final chapter will give you more insight into this powerful strategy that will help you stay motivated as you work towards achieving your goals.

CHAPTER 15:

ONE STEP AT A TIME: CELEBRATE YOUR SMALL WINS

"The great victory, which appears so simple today, was the result of a series of small victories that went unnoticed."
—Paulo Coelho

Successful people don't write down their vision today and see it manifest tomorrow. I know that everyone reading this understands that, but please bear with me—I'm trying to make a point. My first book was around 100,000 words long and divided into 12 chapters. I wrote the book over six months. I only celebrated when I had finished writing the book. Each completed chapter was a small win, but I didn't celebrate any of those small wins because I didn't see them as wins. As far as I was concerned, the only win worth celebrating was when I had finished writing the book. I'm not mad at myself, because back then, I had no idea about the concept of small wins. But what I've learned is that small wins will motivate you to keep going. It's like when you get lost on your way somewhere because you accidentally took the wrong turning. The road suddenly looks unfamiliar, but as you keep driving, and turning into different streets, the area starts looking familiar. You notice the old post box on the left, the school further down on the right, and the lamppost outside the church with a piece of red string hanging off it. All of these signs give you hope that you're on the right track and that you'll arrive at your destination shortly. Celebrating small wins motivates you to keep going. Every milestone you complete is a sign that you'll soon reach your goal. Let's talk about celebrating small wins.

What Exactly Are Small Wins?

Arnold Schwarzenegger said, "Look for small victories and build on that. Each small victory, even if it is just getting up five minutes earlier, gives you confidence. You realize that these little victories make you feel great and keep going. You realize that being paralyzed by fear of failure is worse than failure."

Let's say that one of your goals is to join the 5:00 a.m. club so you can go to the gym every morning before work. You try for a week but keep hitting the snooze button even though you've been going to bed earlier to make up for the two hours' sleep you would lose. One of the things you've learned on your personal development journey is not to take big leaps when it comes to changing your behavior because the mind can't handle it and will force you back into your old habits. So, instead, you decide to break the challenge up into 15-minute increments one week at a time. On the first week, you set your alarm clock for 6:45 a.m., and instead of going to the gym, you run on the spot for 15 minutes and then get ready for work. You find this relatively easy to do and you manage to wake up at 6:45 a.m. for seven days in a row and jog on the spot for 15 minutes. The second week, you set your alarm for 6:30 a.m. You wake up, jog on the spot, and do some strength-training exercises. You manage to do this for a week, and then every week until you are easily waking up at 5:00 a.m. Instead of giving up on your goal, you trained your body to get used to waking up earlier for four weeks, and now you're a pro. Every day you were able to wake up fifteen minutes earlier was a small win because it led up to the big win of waking up at 5:00 a.m.

In general, people don't celebrate small wins because they seem insignificant in comparison to the overall goal. It seems silly calling your friend up to celebrate waking up 15 minutes early when you're still such a long way off from waking up at 5:00 a.m. It might seem silly, but it's not, because you're training your subconscious mind to ditch bad habits and make room for the good habits. Each day you get out of bed when the alarm goes off, your confidence grows because you're seeing progress. With each step you take, suddenly your goal doesn't seem so unrealistic after all.

In a study conducted by the University of Sheffield in the United Kingdom, it was discovered there was a strong relationship between monitoring progress and goal attainment. What the researchers found was that celebrating small wins encouraged intrinsic motivation. Small wins boost your self-esteem and make you feel good about yourself. While the small win is an achievement, the real achievement is the confidence booster, because now you're actually starting to believe you can achieve your goals. Let's look a little deeper into this.

You set a goal to get your house in order because you want to become more organized. Remember, in Chapter 5 I said that your identity is connected to your goals. So, now you want to view yourself as an organized person who has all their ducks in a row. Several months ago, you bought a beautiful piece of wall art that's been sitting on the floor for quite some time. You hang it up. That's a small win, so you celebrate it. To the outsider looking in, it might seem like nothing—what's so impressive about banging a nail into a wall and hanging a picture up? But to you, it's massive because you have no hand-eye coordination, you had to watch several YouTube videos to teach you the right way to hang a picture up, and it took you about two hours to complete the task. Now, each time you walk into your living room and see the picture hanging up on the wall, you feel extremely proud of yourself because it looks good, and you did it. Even though it took you several months to hang the picture up, you said you were going to do it, and you did it—which makes you trust yourself more and gives you the feeling that you can depend on yourself. As you slowly start tidying up your house, you have more mental energy because you're freeing up space in your subconscious mind about all the things you need to get done. Every closet you clear, every pile of papers you organize, and every stray item you give a home clears up more and more space in your subconscious mind. It's not just about the clutter, but about how you feel each time you achieve a milestone. That feeling of relief that you've finally done it, coupled with the boost in self-confidence is extremely important.

Many of your small wins are habits you are developing that have a positive effect on every area of your life. With every small win, you are subconsciously saying to yourself, "I am becoming…"—*[fill in the blank.]* Developing confidence in yourself is essential to achieving your goals because no matter how much anyone *else* believes in you, if you don't believe in *yourself*, you will never achieve anything. What do you think about the friend who is always late? That you can never depend on them to be on time. What do you think about the friend who can never keep a secret? That you can never depend on them to keep your private business to themselves. So, what do you think about *yourself* when you're constantly setting goals and you never achieve them? That you're incapable of achieving your goals.

When you have no faith in yourself, it's literally impossible to become successful. But when that friend tells you they're turning over a new leaf and they're going to stop being late, you don't take them seriously until they actually stop being late. The first time it happens, you don't think too much about it. But the second, third, fourth, and fifth time they're on time, you go, "Wait a minute—*[insert friend's name]* might actually be serious about this." The more they show up on time, the more your faith in them is restored and you start trusting them. The same with your gossipy friend, and the same with you. That's why tracking your progress and celebrating your small wins is so important.

How to Celebrate Your Small Wins

One of the things on my to-do list a couple of years back was to climb Mount Kilimanjaro. I was really excited—until I arrived at the bottom of the mountain and saw how gigantic it was. I immediately started panicking because I was like, "There's no way on earth I'm going to be able to do this." I had to talk myself into not quitting. The only way to shake my fear was to crack on and take the first step. There were several milestones along the way, and each time the group arrived at one, we celebrated by high-fiving each other, hugging, singing, and laughing. When we turned around and looked down the mountain, we were in complete awe at how far we'd come. Each milestone we reached helped us overcome the feeling of wanting to give up. That's how we made it to the top. But humans are obsessed with only celebrating when we get to the top. When it comes to your small wins, decide which milestones you will celebrate along the way.

It's the small wins that build resilience and mental toughness. It took courage for us to climb to the top of Mount Kilimanjaro; it was the most difficult thing I've ever done. There were plenty of setbacks along the way. My partner got sick, and we had to camp for a couple of days until she got better. I twisted my ankle, so we had to camp for a couple of days until the swelling went down. The journey to the top of the mountain should have taken nine days—instead, it took 21 days. Trust me, we thought about quitting many times, but we gritted our teeth and persevered. We became different people when we got to the top. It was the most awesome feeling in the world. From that moment onwards, we knew we could accomplish anything. Success is about doing everything humanly possible to achieve your goals, and the person you become as you make your way there.

I struggle with celebrating small wins because I'm always looking at the bigger picture. If I'm writing a 100,000-word book, and I've only written one chapter—which is typically around 10,000 words—my mind automatically goes to the 90,000 words I've got to finish and not the 10,000 words I've completed. I'm less concerned about the small block that I've chipped off. But I've had to train myself to celebrate these milestones, and I'll typically do something like allow myself to watch several episodes of one of my favorite Netflix shows (and there are many), buy myself something nice, have a couple of glasses of wine, or take myself out to dinner. Your celebration doesn't need to be anything grand or expensive—just make sure you acknowledge your progress. I've made a habit of telling my partner anytime I reach a milestone. Not because I want recognition and a pat on the back, but it's my way of saying out loud that I'm proud of myself, and it's also a nice way of inviting my partner into the process. Celebrate your wins however you want to *celebrate them*. The bottom line is, *celebrate them*. But here are a few tips:

- Give yourself some tender love and care with a home spa, a bubble bath, a face mask and a glass of wine.
- Order yourself something from Amazon.
- Go on a staycation.
- Cook your favorite meal.
- Do something you've never done before.
- Go to the movies.
- Go to the theater.
- Have a professional photoshoot.
- Eat some candy.
- Eat junk food.

I have a lot of fun celebrating my small wins because I never know how I will celebrate until I've reached the milestone. I have a "small wins jar," and it's filled with hundreds of strips of paper with celebratory ideas written on them. When I pull one out, I put it in another jar until the first is empty and then start again. You should try it.

CONCLUSION

"The path to success is to take massive, determined, actions."
—Tony Robbins

And speaking of small wins, congratulate yourself on finishing this book! One of the most annoying habits my friends and I had was our inability to finish reading books. As I mentioned in Chapter 11, we would get all excited about a new get-rich-quick scheme and buy loads of books about it. We'd read the first couple of chapters and quickly realize that this scheme wasn't going to make us rich overnight, and the books would end up collecting dust on our shelves. So, the fact that you've actually got to the conclusion is a testament to your determination to succeed. Now you have the knowledge, it's about applying it.

When I was young, my parents always told me to respect the elderly because they were full of wisdom. While I agree we are to respect the elderly, it shouldn't be because they are full of wisdom—because the reality is that a lot of old people are not wise. Wisdom is the application of knowledge, and when that knowledge is applied, you see the results in a person's life. As the saying goes, "You know a tree by the fruit that it bears." A lot of old people I spoke to when I was younger, and still to this day, are full of knowledge, but they are not wise because they have never applied it. Remember I told you in the introduction about Mr. Hamilton? He knew exactly how to how become successful, but he didn't apply it. Although I appreciated his advice and respected him for his accumulation of knowledge, I couldn't respect him for being full of wisdom, because he wasn't.

What am I trying to tell you? Don't be like Mr. Hamilton, 70 years old, sitting on your porch, advising the youth to follow their dreams and to not turn out like you. Whatever you want to achieve, the power is in your action. Achieving your goals is dependent upon the work you do. I believe that anything is possible for those who are willing to work hard to turn their dreams into reality. What you want out of life will never be handed to you on a plate—it's up to you to go out there and take it. Because we live in a microwave society where everyone wants everything immediately, a lot of people will invest a couple of weeks, maybe months in visualizing, meditating, and writing out their goals. But when they don't see it manifest within the timeframe they had envisioned, they give up. I used to be one of those people. I knew I needed to write my books myself, but I truly believed that doing these things would somehow give me the motivation I needed to start writing. They never did. I had to learn how to motivate myself and take action.

I can't tell you this journey is going to be easy because that would be very dishonest of me. Achieving your goals is the most difficult thing you will ever do, and it will take everything you've got. Letting go of your friends is probably the most painful part of the process. I can guarantee you will lose your friends when you start working on your goals. Author John Maxwell said, "It's lonely at the top, so you better know why you're there." Actor Charlie Sheen said, "People say it's lonely at the top, but I sure like the view." And influencer Gary Vee said, "It's lonely at the top. If you don't like that, then don't start a company." Let me repeat: you are going to lose your friends as you start your ascent. If you want to hang on to a group of people who don't have the drive to succeed, kiss your dreams goodbye—because it's impossible to carry dead weight to the top. Your friends are either going to leave you, or you'll leave them.

Once you've got your vision down on paper and broken it down into small, manageable chunks, don't waste any time. Get to work immediately—because the longer you leave it, the harder it will be to get started. And once you start, don't look back. Make a decision *right now* that this will be your last day of inaction. Life is too short not to fulfil your mission on earth. You are here for a reason; don't go to your grave without finding out what it is. Many people allow fear to hold them back. They have a fear of failure, a fear of what other people will think, a fear of stepping out of their comfort zone. Fear is poison; it will infest every area of your life and keep you locked in the prison of inaction. Don't let it hold you captive. It's natural to be afraid when you're going against the grain and refusing to conform to the norms and values of society. But courageous people feel the fear and do it anyway. If you allow fear to hold you back, you will never know whether your dreams were possible, and you'll live with that regret until the end of your days.

I believe in you, and I'm cheering you on as you turn your dreams into reality. I wish you every success as you climb to the top of the mountain!

THANKS FOR READING!

If this book has helped you in any way, pass it on to other people you know are struggling to take action to achieve their goals.

Also, can you do me a huge favor and leave a review on Amazon? Reviews help people like yourself who want to change their lives decide whether this is the right book for them. Thank you so much in advance.

Simply find this book on Amazon, scroll to the reviews section, and click "Write a customer review".

Or alternatively please visit www.pristinepublish.com/actionreview to leave a review.

Be sure to check out my email list, where I am constantly adding tons of value. The best way to currently get on the list is by visiting www.pristinepublish.com/morningbonus and entering your email address.

Here, I'll provide actionable information that aims to improve your enjoyment of life. I'll update you on my latest books, and I'll even send free e-books that I think you'll find useful.

Kindest regards,
Daniel Walter

Also by
Daniel Walter

Discover the Secrets to Self-Discipline Today.

Visit: www.pristinepublish.com/danielbooks

REFERENCES

Amabile, T., & Kramer, S. (2011) *The Progress Principle: Using Small Wins to Ignite Joy, Engagement, and Creativity at Work.* Harvard Business Press.

American Psychological Association (2006). *Multitasking: Switching costs.*

Arabdotorg (n.d.). *Study: It Pays to Be Generous*

Becker, J. (2018) *The Minimalist Home: A Room-by-Room Guide to a Decluttered, Refocused Life.* WaterBrook.

Bonney, A. (2019) *Get Over It: 47 tips for Embracing the Discomfort of Change.* Anne Bonney Enterprises

Bradt, S. (2010). *Wandering mind not a happy mind.* Harvard Gazette.

Burns, C. (2014) *Instant Motivation: The Surprising Truth Behind What Really Drives Top Performance.* Pearson UK.

Campbell, B., & Manning, J. (2018) *The Rise of Victimhood Culture: Microaggressions, Safe Spaces, and the New Culture Wars.* Springer.

Canfield, J. (2012) *The Success Principles.* Harper Collins

CDC (2023). *Heart disease facts. Centers for Disease Control and Prevention*

Chowdhury, M.R. (2019). *A Look at the Psychology of Goal Setting (Incl. 3 Research Findings). PositivePsychology.*

Clear, J. (2018) *Atomic Habits: The Life-changing Million-copy #1 Bestseller.* Random House.

Clutterbuck, D. (2003) *Managing Work-life Balance: A Guide for HR in Achieving Organisational and Individual Change.* CIPD Publishing.

Corley, T. C. (2010) *Rich Habits: The Daily Success Habits of Wealthy Individuals.* Hillcrest Publishing Group.

Cousins, L. (2017). *Why 'bottling it up' can be harmful to your health | HCF.*

DeBoskey, B. (n.d.). *Philanthropy helps the giver, too.* The Detroit News.

Dyer, W. W. (1991) *Pulling Your Own Strings: Dynamic Techniques for Dealing with Other People and Living Your Life As You Choose.* Harper Collins.

Ferrari, M. D., & Sternberg, R. J. (1998) *Self-awareness: Its Nature and Development.* Guilford Press.

Forrest, L., & Meagher, E. (2011) *Guiding Principles for Life Beyond Victim Consciousness.* Conscious Living Media

Fritz, R. S. (1986) *The Path of Least Resistance.* Random House

Goggins, D. (2020) *Can't Hurt me: Master Your Mind and Defy the Odds – Clean Edition.* Lioncrest Publishing

Harrison, K. R. (2014) *Victors and Victims: Are you Being Held Back by a Victim Mentality?* Authentic Media Inc.

Hill, N. (2005) *Think and Grow Rich: The Landmark Bestseller Now Revised and Updated for the 21st Century.* Penguin.

Hurst, M. (2023). *Why you should try the 12-12-12 decluttering method.*

King T. (2022). *What's the 20/20 rule for decluttering? Professional organizers explain.*

Kondo, M. (2015) *The Life-changing Magic of Tidying Up: The Japanese Art of Decluttering and Organizing.* Thorndike Press.

Kushner, H. S. (2007) *Overcoming Life's Disappointments: Learning from Moses How to Cope with Frustration.* Anchor.

Levitin, D. (2015) *The Organized Mind: Thinking Straight in the Age of Information Overload.* Penguin UK.

Lively, D. L. (2012) *How to Recognize and Overcome Victim Mentality: Learn Why Taking Responsibility Is the Most Important Step to Your Health and Well-Being and the Steps to Take to Open the Door to Anything You Desire.* Createspace Independent Pub.

Markel, G., PhD. (2013) *Actions Against Distractions: Managing Your Scattered, Disorganized, and Forgetful Mind.* Manage Your Mind LLC

McQueen, M. (2016) *Momentum: How to Build it, Keep it or Get it Back.* John Wiley & Sons.

Meadows, M. (2017) *365 Days with Self-Discipline: 365 Life-Altering Thoughts on Self-Control, Mental Resilience, and Success.* Meadows Publishing.

Mental Health Org. (n.d.). *Kindness matters guide.*

Milosevic, Y. (2020). *Fight Distractions to Stretch Your Attention Span.* The Blacklight.

Nast, C. (2018). *Here's scientific proof your brain was designed to be distracted.* Wired UK.

Newport Institute. (2021). *The Scary Truth About How Zombie Scrolling Impacts Mental Health.*

Perna, M.C. (n.d.). *Why Employees Hate Their Jobs—And 6 Ways To Change That.* Forbes.

Psychologies (2021). *Music makes you feel better.* Psychologies.

Review, H. B., Goleman, D., Kaplan, R. S., David, S., & Eurich, T. (2018) *Self-Awareness (HBR Emotional Intelligence Series).* Harvard Business Press.

Sample, I. (2010). *Living in the moment really does make people happier.* The Guardian.

Schwartz, A.E. (2001) *Goal-Setting: Target Your Achievement.* Andrew E Schwartz.

Tracy, B (2009). Success Through Goal Setting, Part 1 of 3. Brian Tracy.

Ware, B. (2012) *The Top Five Regrets of the Dying: A Life Transformed by the Dearly Departing.* Hay House Incorporated.

Ways, O. N., & Jane, L. (2018) *Cleaning and Organization Hacks – Simple House Cleaning Hacks to Minimize Clutter and Stay Organized Easily.* Fastlane LLC

Wen, T. (2020). *The 'law' that explains why you can't get anything done.* BBC

Printed in Great Britain
by Amazon